ESSENTIAL
SPORT COACHING
PRINCIPLES

LEARN - COACH - PERFORM

A guide for those new and newer to sport coaching

ISBN: 978-1-7643286-0-9

Table of Contents

Welcome to Coaching

The aim of this book is to provide practical and applied information to coaches who are perhaps new to the art and science of coaching, or those with experience who are looking to expand their knowledge.

I will explain various non-sport specific concepts in athlete preparation with the minimum use of jargon. Where technical terms are required, they will be explained beforehand. Sometimes it may seem like an oversimplification of the art and science of sport coaching, but that is deliberately done to ensure readers with minimal experience can benefit.

I commenced coaching in various sports in the mid-1970's, whilst still at school, where I "Captain/coached" the high school badminton team, then coached the school senior softball team, before coaching club softball with my sport coaching life continuing for over 30 years in various sports. To further my coaching knowledge, I continued in tertiary education to complete a Masters in Sport Coaching at the University of Queensland.

A question I often hear is "Why bother learning about coaching? I played the sport, so I know I can coach". My answer is that "Sure, you may know the sport, which may make you OK as a game day coach, but what do you know about physical and emotional athlete preparation, skill acquisition, recovery, session/weekly/seasonal/ long-term athlete development planning?"

If the above sounds too complex, remember, a parent/caregiver is entrusting you to develop their child to be the best that they can be; to nurture their development; to teach them the required skills in an appropriate, planned and progressive way; to keep them engaged and not damage them physically or psychologically.

As a "newer" coach, you're often given beginner athletes. I've never understood a novice coach in charge of novice athletes. Novice athletes are a "blank slate", so everything you do will be fundamental to their development. You are effectively laying the foundation that supports their athletic career, and we all know what a poor foundation can lead to. One movement error that is learned can lead to under-performance or injury, as well as potentially years of retraining to correct the movement. Push too hard and they may disengage due to physical and/or psychological overload, not hard enough and they also may disengage as they're not getting the development they expect, and conclude that you may not care. Just to add to the complexity, it is unlikely that you will have a homogeneous group under your management, so there will be a broad range of needs to understand. Interestingly, the more advanced athletes tend to become more homogeneous in some areas.

This book will not pretend to cover all aspects of coaching. What I hope to achieve is to give you a basic but useful and applied understanding to increase your confidence to deliver sound outcomes for your athletes. Hopefully, I will also spark your enthusiasm to continue to learn more.

By reading this book, you've already demonstrated your desire to improve as a sports coach. I wish you well in your coaching endeavours.

What does being a Coach mean?

In its most basic form, the role of the coach is to control and manage the coordinated and integrated processes that achieve the goals/aspirations of an athlete/team. This role definition places the coach in a leadership position. It also identifies that coaching is an ongoing process and not an episodic or 'one-off' event, implying a long-term association with the athlete/team's ongoing development.

Task: Do you see yourself as a participation, development, or performance coach? Why?

A participation coach is one where your athletes are not involved in competition at a high level. These coaches are usually within a recreational sporting context, which is characterised by low intensities, short-term goals with limited performance elements. A development coach is involved with coaching in a competition based sports program, mostly coaching age-group athletes who are aspiring performance athletes. A performance coach operates within a more formal structure with clubs/squads and implements more elements of the coaching process.

Task: With the above definitions, do you now see yourself as a participation, development, or performance coach?

Roles of a Coach

There are three fundamental roles to being a coach:

1. Developing athletes to become self-reliant and self-directed in their development.
2. To be the "go-between" by aligning your program and your athlete's goals.
3. To produce athletes with predictable physical and psychological performances.

Using the above three roles, we can identify the basic building blocks that encapsulate coaching:

- Identify the athlete's needs.
- Develop a development/intervention strategy to meet the athlete's needs.
- Design and deliver practice based upon the developed strategy.
- Analyse and critique the outcomes of the delivered practice.
- Use the analysis/critique to inform future practice design and delivery.

The above is a broad brush stroke of what is generally seen as coaching; however, the coach is dealing with people all the time, so the quality of the interpersonal relationships are critical to success as it impacts all areas within the coach's scope.

I mentioned above that one of the fundamental roles of the coach was to increase the predictability of the athlete's performance (or alternately to reduce the unpredictability of performance). The nature of the relationship between the coach and athlete should not be underestimated in its influence on athlete performance predictability. The interpersonal relationship can affect the athlete's emotional state, motivation, identity, and engagement.

Coaching Styles – a brief overview

Task: Cast your mind back to when you were being coached – what coaching style did you perform best under? Did your preferred style change as you got older or as your focus shifted towards performance?

There are two opposing coaching styles, each at the extreme ends of the coaching style spectrum – authoritative and democratic, with a floating scale connecting them. The key descriptors for each style are:

- Authoritative: directive, coach-led, task-oriented, outcome focused.
- Democratic: interactive, athlete-led, person-oriented, process-focused.

It is unlikely that a coach is either authoritative or democratic in their pure forms, but the coach uses elements from each in varying degrees to define their coaching style. The coach's style is also most likely to vary depending upon the level or developmental stage the athletes are at, and may also vary from a context standpoint (practice vs competition).

When coaching new/newer athletes, it is more likely that the coaching style would lean towards an authoritative style, where the coach is the sole decision maker, is the sole provider of information and teaching, determines the standards, and exhibits rigidity in behaviour.

As athletes progress in competence and understanding, the coaching style often changes to be more democratic. This is exhibited by the athletes being a part of the decision-making process, the communication becomes two-way between the coach and the athlete, with associated active engagement of the athlete, with a greater emphasis placed on the interpersonal relationship. This is also referred to as a humanist approach.

As already stated, the applied coaching style is unlikely to be at either end, but somewhere along the connective line between them.

> **Task**: What are the advantages and disadvantages of the two coaching styles?

An authoritarian coach's athletes tend to exhibit higher levels of anxiety; however, they do feel that their training environment is well organised and that they are physically well prepared. At the opposite end of coaching styles (democratic style), we find a coach who is flexible and shows a high level of concern and consideration for their athletes, resulting in a relaxed low pressure environment, however, the coach may come across to their athletes as having a weak personality.

Although each coach brings their existing personality traits with them, which have been developed through their own experiences and education, it is important for the coach to spend time in self-analysis to determine what traits they exhibit and the potential impact those traits may have on different athletes' engagement, enjoyment, and performance.

Once traits and the possible effects on athletes have been identified, the coach can consciously work to ensure that they develop a flexibility of coaching styles dependent upon the athlete/s they are coaching at that moment, whilst remaining true to their own values.

A coaching paradigm

Coaching is not just a simplistic matter of the coach providing a stimulus to the athlete to elicit a response leading to performance improvement and adaptation, because coaching is rather more multifaceted than a simple "input-output" linear structure.

As coaches, you are working with athletes who may be at varying chronological, developmental, and training ages and also prefer different communication styles, have varying needs within the inter-personal relationship with the coach etc, which places a greater range of understanding and interaction requirements upon the coach. This leads me to suggest that coaches should apply a holistic view to their work, utilising humanistic coaching practices.

To coach under a humanist umbrella means that the coach allows and facilitates personal growth and development of the individual athlete by ensuring a positive environment for engagement, self-determination, improvement, and achievement.

Through this model, the coach incrementally empowers the athlete to move from a coach controlled environment (coach dependant – early stage athlete; perhaps under 12 years of age) along to a shared coach/athlete controlled environment (developing a more coach/athlete collaborative environment; move towards athlete self management; shared decision making – perhaps 12-18 years old), and finally an athlete controlled environment (athlete has greater independence and autonomy; exhibits self-responsibility).

To progress from a coach-controlled to a collaborative environment, the coach needs to understand the individual athlete through providing appropriate communication and motivation, and by exhibiting consistent personal behaviours.

For coaches to give themselves permission to facilitate the movement of an athlete into a coach/athlete collaborative environment and then onto an athlete-controlled environment can be very difficult, as often the coach can believe that they are making themselves redundant, or empowering the athlete to possibly leave their program. My view is if the coach believes this to be the case, then they should go back to the start and remind themselves as to why they commenced coaching in the first place.

In my own coaching experience, to facilitate the movement of athletes towards a collaborative environment, I educated them in basic exercise physiology and how the session program relates to their performance development, and how it sits within the periodised structure. Questions from athletes were always encouraged and answered using language that was appropriate to their education level at that time so they could understand the answer.

In conclusion, the coach may want to follow the athlete development line from coach-controlled to athlete-controlled stringently, however, that is not realistic in all circumstances. Most sports require the coach and athlete/s to operate within a blended environment to be successful. For example, in a team sport, the coach may involve athletes in program design and the athlete/s may self-manage some elements (recovery, nutrition etc), but on game day, it is likely that the tactics/plays will be coach-led.

Communication

You were probably thinking that I would start with what many people believe coaching is about, possibly the physiological preparation of an athlete to perform, or something similar. I agree that it is one of the fundamental components of coaching, but if you can't get your information across to the intended audience, your effectiveness will be demonstrably diminished. Let's take a moment to think about who our audience is.

> **TASK**: Make a short list of who you think your audience could be. The audience members of your list may vary depending on your coaching situation and may differ from my list, which is below.

My list (in no specific order of importance): parents/caregivers; athletes; sport officials at events; club committee; sponsors; media (eg. social media feed; local news media); venue or stadium management; equipment suppliers; funding/sponsorship organisations; team manager; fellow coaches; if at a higher level this may also include a strength and conditioning coach, physiotherapist, psychologist, exercise physiologist, biomechanist, etc.

I'd like to discuss a few of what I believe to be the key audience members that you will engage with as a new coach.

Parents/Caregivers

Over the years, I've spoken to many coaches about communicating with this group, often met with either an eye-roll, stories of frustration, or indifference. I cannot stress this highly enough – this group is fundamental to not only your success but also to how enjoyable your coaching time will be. Let's briefly investigate what I mean.

How can a parent/caregiver be fundamental to your success? After all, they're not the athlete. Assuming you are coaching juniors, a parent/caregiver will perform the following tasks, without which you cannot coach. They will:

- bring your athlete to training and competitions
- feed your athlete
- ensure your athlete is rested and ready
- assist your athlete in recovery and injury management
- be a source of information about their child (how they learn, what type of issues they may have, what type of reward/encouragement they respond to, etc)
- provide a supportive home environment
- pay your fees, and/or club fees
- pay for your athletes' competition fees and travel expenses
- pay for all the personal equipment the athlete needs
- devote time
- support you and your vision/plan behind the scenes

If you coach "seniors", they may drive themselves to training and competitions, they may even fund themselves if they are working, but if they are living at home, many of the above elements still hold. If they are living independently, they still may need information from you for some of the above identified points.

Engagement

Now we've established that the parent/caregiver is fundamental to your program, how best to engage with them? That in itself is a broad question, as like all people, this group is not homogeneous in makeup; there are variances in personality, general engagement, drive, and communication style. I'm sure you can readily think of people you know within this group who are very different. This is a good thing. Differences bring diversity of thinking, goals, and education which may challenge you in discussions with them and broaden your approach. It is also possible that this diversity of opinion/attitude etc is reflected in their child, which can give you an insight into athlete management.

Newer coaches tend to keep a distance from the parent/caregiver, often due to fear of the unknown, perhaps being fearful of not being able to answer a question satisfactorily, or they have a lack of confidence.

I've encountered many different parent/caregivers in my years of coaching. Some are indifferent and simply want their child to do "something", others are more engaged. I've had sceptical parent/caregivers who need to be given information so they can understand what your thinking is with their child's development. I've also had parents who were exercise physiologists ask about my program and how their child fits in (of course, they don't walk up and tell you their background upfront). So you can never really be sure what knowledge a parent/caregiver has. Do you think that is a concern you could have?

Let's attempt to address some of these concerns.

We've established that the parent/caregiver is fundamental to your program/coaching and that they need to be engaged with and not shied away from. Being a new coach can come with advantages, namely that everyone involved knows you're at an embryonic stage of your coaching career and that you will make mistakes. You're still learning from a basic start point. The hope, is of course, that any mistakes you make are not damaging to anyone (physically or psychologically), that you only make the mistake once, and most importantly, you recognise, acknowledge, take ownership of your mistake or misstep, don't diminish its importance, and learn from it.

Task: How would you go about meeting the parent/caregiver of either a new athlete to your program, or your commencement as a coach? What topics would you cover in that conversation? Would it be a different conversation depending on different age groups?

We've all heard the expression "first impressions count". I would add a caveat to that, and that is the first meeting must show who you are, the genuine and authentic you. If you put on a facade because that may be how you think you want to be perceived or what you believe to be the expectations of your audience, you will be found out. Be yourself within the context of being a coach.

Let me provide a real example from my coaching (the sport was a field sport). Grant funding was made available to run a "high performance" program for U17's, male. The first program commenced 9 am on a Sunday at a sports park. I arrived at 8:15 to commence setup of cones for warm-up and running work of 90 minutes duration. I had already written the program, timed to the minute. Parents/caregivers arrived soon after with the athletes and observed me setting up. How often have you seen coaches stepping out distances between cones? Does "close enough" set the standard you expect? I used a tape measure, cones at 5, 10, 20, 25 metre distances, which were all accurate to the centimetre, as were gaps between mini-hurdles. Do you expect accuracy from your athletes? I do, so I set myself the same standard. Be genuine – don't expect behaviours from athletes you don't yourself exhibit. Athletes will quickly recognise this disingenuous behaviour, and you may lose their respect, or you may undermine your program.

Before the start, I addressed everyone as a group, introducing myself, stating the objectives of the program and what the goals for the day's session would be. After the session, I debriefed the athletes' as a group, and then made myself openly available to the parent/caregivers to answer any of their questions or just have a general chat. Only after that did I pack up the equipment. Coaches are the first to arrive and the last to leave.

Do you think the above is excessive? The first meeting with a new group allows you to immediately set the standards and expectations and start to build the culture you want for your program. It is easier to establish this from the start than to build it over time. Once started, you must be able to maintain it. It is a pressure you put on yourself to perform.

Criticism

Criticism from parents/caregivers. Yes, it will occur, guaranteed. Could it be justified – possibly. But how to handle this, how do you react? Your attitude, behaviour, and language (both body and verbal) will be critical to the outcome of any such conversation. Also, the athlete may also be standing there, listening and observing you.

Task: You've been coaching a group of newer athletes for a few weeks, and a parent/caregiver approaches you and is unhappy about the skill level their child has achieved compared with others. How do you react? Write down a short list of your thoughts,

> emotional response, what you would say, and perhaps what you
> wouldn't say.

Let's think about your emotional response first. How does this make you feel, and then how do you react to those emotions?

The parent/caregivers query may or may not be valid to you. But it is valid to them. The fact that they are posing the query to you shows that they are engaged, which surely is a good thing. But do you suddenly feel under siege? Ready to "raise the drawbridge" or just give coaching away? Good. Emotional attachment demonstrates you care. Let's consider your emotional control first and how that influences the conversation.

Keep your voice under control and don't use defensive or aggressive language, irrespective of what's coming your way. Listen actively, paraphrase the query to help you understand what's been said (paraphrasing also allows you to break down the query into smaller manageable chunks allowing you to control the conversation focus, allows time to "breathe", can deescalate and lower emotions) which also lets the person with the query know you are listening and taking it seriously. Note: I'm referring to this as a "query", not a "complaint". This allows you to have a different emotional perspective on the conversation.

After you've fully understood the query, take your time to formulate a considered response; don't just blurt out the first thing that comes into your head. Be honest in your response. If you haven't noticed, say so, and add that you will revisit your program delivery to better meet the needs of individuals. Be encouraging to them and say you are open to receiving queries (although they may call it a complaint, and don't say something like "thanks for your query/complaint", as that can come across as patronising), as that will only help with your coaching development, as you are still relatively new to coaching. Advise them that you have a solution or will develop one that you will incorporate into your program to benefit all athletes. Perhaps you will seek guidance from a more experienced coach. Ensure they are fully aware of what action plan you will put in place. And above all, do it! Don't recognise the query as valid, provide a verbal solution, and then not carry it out.

But what if the query/complaint lacks validity? This comes under the umbrella of parent/caregiver education. Same as the above scenario, actively listen, and paraphrase when appropriate to ensure you really understand what they are saying. Again, don't be defensive. You should know the athlete. Explain where you believe the athlete is at currently in a clear and precise manner. Above all, don't speak down to the parent/caregiver, or use jargon/technical language the parent/caregiver may not understand in an attempt to appear "clever", it's not a game of oneupmanship or to demonstrate how smart you are. In this scenario, I would explain to them where the athlete's development currently sits, where it has developed recently, and where I expect it to develop. I would also point out any difficulties the athlete is demonstrating and strategies I would implement (and have been implementing) to address them. For example, it may be that they missed out on some fundamental development work (although careful here – don't refer to or blame any historic coaching they may have received as you want to ensure the conversation remains positive and about the here and now) which you are addressing, but it has necessitated the athlete taking a step back to address those first before moving forward, as in the longer term it will yield a superior movement/skill etc than would most likely have occurred.

These scenarios give the parent/caregiver an understanding in several areas: you have identified an issue and have a plan to address it; you know the athlete; you care about the long term development of the athlete to reach their potential; or you are prepared to acknowledge what you don't know and will seek advice; you are approachable.

It may also be that the query relates to a disparity of performance between their child and others. In this case, you need to provide concise information about the differences between developmental (maturation) age, training age (how many years of training), and chronological age (actual calendar-based age). These three parameters can lead to a differential in performance and skill acquisition. It can also be the case that at some point an athlete will hit a difficulty in learning a skill effectively and may need a different approach or drills to assist them in that skill acquisition. You do need to be aware of these issues as they relate to each athlete so that you can speak with knowledge and authority to the parent/caregiver, as well as engage with the athlete so they know you have a plan for their development.

Be proactive. By that, I mean don't be afraid to approach the parent/caregiver before they approach you with your observations about their child. Opening a conversation may seem difficult and confronting, but it's not if you have the provable facts from your subjective and objective observations and approach the conversation using positive language together with an action plan.

For example, you've noticed an athlete (let's call the athlete "Jane") is slow to react to a starting signal for a race, and it's holding back her performance. So before you are approached by a concerned parent/caregiver, you decide to approach them. How would you do that? Please give it a thought for a moment, then read on. Remember, not one solution fits all situations.

Try to catch up with the parent/caregiver before training and ask if they could spare a few minutes after training for a catch-up. They mustn't be caught by surprise. Ensure the catch-up is in a space where a confidential conversation can take place. Also, remember that Jane may also be there. So how would you start the conversation?

There are two basic options (both abbreviated from what a real conversation would be like).

Option 1: may commence something like this, "Jane like all athletes has a lot to learn on their pathway (I hate the word "journey", it's so overused, and pathway implies a mapped out progression) and I've noticed Jane takes a while to respond to a 'Go' stimulus and that's something I would like to focus on improving in the short term and may need your help. Jane and I have already spoken about this, and she's keen to get extra help". (Wait for their response to see how engaged they are, or they may even be able to provide you with additional information about Jane). Assuming engagement and no additional information is forthcoming, then explain your intervention strategy. As an example, this may involve practising falling starts, or starts from a stimulus, which can also be practised at home, and perhaps a dropped ruler drill. (dropping a ruler between finger and thumb and measuring how many centimetres/inches pass by before the finger/thumb closes and stops the ruler). This may sound bizarre to a new coach, but it provides cognitive processing with reflex action, which is measurable without specialised equipment. The conversation concludes by ensuring Jane understands what's being proposed – always include the athlete as an active member of the conversation, no matter what age they are.

Option 2: "Jane has an issue with responding to a 'Go' stimulus, and I'm not sure if she just isn't concentrating or what, but it's holding her back. Jane needs to focus on improving that. I just wanted to let you know what I'm seeing at training".

Which do you think would be a more successful discussion and why?

The second option, albeit a shorter conversation, importantly lays the blame on Jane for non-performance and offers no solutions. The coach also doesn't include Jane in the conversation. In the first option, the coach talks to the identified problem and offers solutions, never once inferring that Jane is part of the problem. You must at all times remember, that the outcomes of your athletes are the outcomes you design, manage, implement, and communicate. They're simply following your instructions, good, indifferent, or below par.

Program Interference

The dread amongst coaches is the interfering parent/caregiver. They're either calling out their instructions to their child during a match or event, countermanding your instructions, doing the opposite of what you recommend (e.g eating an endless supply of sweets or lollies (candy) during an event), or just grumbling on the sidelines, undermining you at every opportunity.

Task: What would you do when the above happens? Perhaps think of possible solutions within each of the above scenarios. What constraints do you have that may limit your actions? What if the athlete involved is your best or key player/athlete – would that alter your response?

Let's set a guiding precedent first. The cornerstone of what you are trying to develop is based foremost on developing and maintaining a specific culture, which you have defined. Do any of these behaviours meet the expectations of that culture? I think that should be your starting point.

I'll mention this several times throughout this book. A significant component of your communication will be non-verbal. Your body language will convey many elements to who you are addressing. Body language includes your stance, your facial expressions, eye movements, arm and hand movements, and posture. The tone of your voice is just as important as the words you choose and how you deliver them. At no time should you endeavour to escalate a conversation to move it to a confrontation. This is counterproductive. Remember, other people (including possibly your athletes) are watching you and their impression of an interaction can be very important to your long-term success. If it goes "pear shaped", the cause of it going "off the rails" may stick with you, even if not justified.

The first thing to do is simple – take a breath and consider your conversation options. Don't go barging in, but take your time to formulate the path you want to control the conversation along. If you are emotional and not calm and relaxed, perhaps reconsider the timing of the conversation.

Although it can be difficult, your emotional control is critical to maintaining control of the conversation. You're a coach, so personal emotional control should be a part of your toolbox.

Depending on where you are, there may be Codes of Conduct that all people involved in the sport must abide by. This includes spectators (including parents/caregivers), officials, administrators, athletes, and of course, coaches. In some circumstances, a committee member may be able to approach the offending person and remind them of the Code they are required to abide by. This may not be a solution available to you, and you may have to tackle the matter yourself.

Task: For each of these scenarios, take a moment to put yourself into the picture and come up with a strategy of how you would handle the situation.

I won't look at every strategy permutation for the above task, but let's go through a couple of the more common possibilities.

Firstly, the "parent/caregiver coaching from the sidelines". I think this is probably the most common issue. Often, the parent/caregiver has been involved in the sport and wants to "contribute". The question you need to ask is this – "Are they deliberately trying to undermine your authority, or are they inadvertently calling out instructions unaware of the impact they are having?" If it's the latter, it's easy to speak with them and advise them that during training or games, the athletes should only be hearing one voice throughout, and that's the coach's. You can say it's confusing for athletes to differentiate between instructions from two sources; it's undermining the role of the coach; however, take on board what they are saying, as it may have validity, and if it does, do tell them that you hear what they are saying, but it is not appropriate during training/games. Extend a hand to them, insofar as you welcome them to provide general information to yourself to assist your learning experience. One swimming coach I knew, invited a parent who has keen to provide "instruction" from the side, to help him in his coaching program as they seem to be very interested in contributing, and then handed them a stopwatch with stroke counter and asked them to stroke count and time each lap of a swimmer (not their child) for a 1500 metre swim. They did, and their sideline contribution stopped after that.

In my own experience, I have rarely had a parent/caregiver offer "coaching" advice to their child, but when they have, I immediately spoke to them. The conversations normally went along the line of: I am working on that aspect with your child as part of their general development but at this moment it's not the focus as I've identified a more important element to refine which will have a positive knock-on effect to their performance, or we will soon be working on that aspect but at the moment this element of focus is of greater need to develop in the kinetic chain which will give your child a "win" in their development. Keep it positive and let them know you are aware of what they are saying, but your current programming priority is 'x', and assure them that their concern will be addressed (assuming those concerns are valid, of course). If it is valid, and you already have the matter programmed in the future, tell them so. Also, politely remind them that at training sessions, the athletes should only be hearing one voice of instruction, and that is the coach's.

The "undermining" parent/caregiver is another matter altogether. If you are the one who must address the situation, you need to be upfront that it's unacceptable and that they must stop. If they ignore you, then the only remedy may be to cut the athlete loose from your program and advise the parent/caregiver that it's an untenable situation and you are no longer prepared to coach their child. This takes a lot of courage for a new coach, and depending on the structure, you may need to speak to a committee first. If you're an independent coach, it's your program and your business to protect. This type of behaviour is toxic to a program, and strong leadership is required to resolve it.

In the above, always remember that emotional control is paramount and not to mirror the other person if they get loud, use aggressive or demeaning language, or invade your personal space. Walk up to them confidently, stand straight, don't fold your arms, don't show behaviours associated with a lack of confidence, such as touching your face, playing with your hair or fidgeting. Don't raise your voice in volume or tenor. If the discussion escalates or they become demeaning, walk away, but calmly point out to them that the discussion is not coming to a conclusion at this point but you would like to continue at a future time to allow time for reflection, and you are therefore terminating it. It allows you to be the controlling agent. Remember, you (as is the parent/caregiver) are most likely being observed by others, including your athletes. Above all, never take the "bait" and "bite" back. Use non-confrontational language and don't become defensive. Make sure you engage early so the issue doesn't grow in influence; in other words, don't avoid the issue. Show your true leadership. You may also be reassured by other parents/caregivers who may manage the matter behind the scenes and support you.

As a word of caution, I would suggest not becoming too friendly with a particular parent/caregiver or sub-group, as it may lead to future conflict within the cohort. At some point, possibly due to athlete selection or perhaps the illusion of favouritism, a perceived real or imaginary friendship may cause you a great deal of issues, so it's best to avoid this potential disruptive scenario from the start. That doesn't mean you can't be amicable, just leave the relationships at a professional level.

As a final point to remember, depending on where in the world you are, there may be cultural differences to how conversations are conducted. These may include speaking to the socially based gender (for example, it may be socially inappropriate for a male coach to speak with a female parent/caregiver and vice-versa); not standing directly in front of someone during conversations, as it may be socially disrespectful, etc. It may be that you are fully aware of the social norms, however, we are becoming more and more multi-cultural, and that will be reflected in your cohort of families so you may need to make yourself familiar with new (to you) specific social norms.

Athletes

As a coach, you are in a position of authority with a power differential between you and the athletes. As a coach, you are not the athlete's friend, and your communication and relationship should reflect that. Athletes look to you for leadership, to provide them with the required or desired athletic development, to support them in their goals, and to provide them with the best you can.

> **Task**: Are you a coach, or are you a teacher? What percentage of time are you either? Would that percentage be different with different age groups or different athletes abilities?

I would suggest that, as a new coach, you will more likely be dealing with newer or younger athletes, so much of your time will be spent teaching.

But let's take a small step back first. How should a coach present themselves? Remember, this is as much about verbal as it is about non-verbal communication.

- Being on time to start, or being early? I suggest being early to allow for setup, to deal with any unexpected issues at the venue, to be able to speak with individual athletes or parent/caregivers (or them to approach you) outside of the actual training time.
- Greet your athletes – those first few words can yield a lot of information about their mental or physical state (are they tired, what is their mood state, are they full of energy, injured, etc).
- Be appropriately attired and groomed. This may sound "old-fashioned", but you are setting the standard and culture you want, if you accept personal sloppiness or tardiness, OK, but don't expect anything different from your athletes. Leaders lead by example.
- Be prepared with your training session designed (and written out).
- Show energy – I don't mean bouncing off the walls as if you're full of red jelly beans, but have energy in your voice, let a feeling of some excitement show through about the training session or game (but not too much, your emotions influence your athletes, but more of that later). Let your athletes feel that you are excited they are there.
- Have good posture, after all, you are a sports coach. It also shows personal confidence which influences others. Believe in yourself - others will believe in you (as long as you can back it up, of course).

Language

The language you choose to use will vary depending on the age group you have in your group. It is a reasonable assumption that the language/words you use when speaking to an 8-year-old athlete will be different from how you speak to a 17-year-old athlete. Beyond maturation differences, the two athletes will have different daily experiences too. These points seem self-explanatory, but must be kept in mind. As athletes mature, so does their language and also how they like to be verbally engaged.

Verbal engagement should be seen as a fundamental to the ongoing relationship development between the coach and their athlete. Depending on the sport or structure, the athlete may be involved in your program for a season, or perhaps ten years or more. The establishment of two-way dialogue builds a communication bridge with a trust foundation, which allows the athlete to have the confidence to broach any subject with you. This is critical in the athlete's development.

Two pronouns often used when addressing athletes:

1. "You", which is a personal pronoun, and

2. "We", which is a subject pronoun

Task: Have you thought about how and when you use them? When instructing an athlete (or a group), do you say "You are going to do ….." or do you say "We are going to do…..?" Think about the tonal difference between them and how they are perceived by the recipient. Further, why not think about how genders (including athletes who are not binary defined) perceive the message.

For the sake of this newer to coaching book and to avoid complexity, I'll use a binary gender definition. You will have to put thought into your communication method and style with your athlete cohort. Always remember, don't be shy to ask the athlete (or the parent/caregiver) how they prefer to be addressed when given instructions.

In my experience, I've found the best results when addressing a male cohort is to use the term "you" when explaining work to be done or times to be made, etc. As in "You are going to run 4 x 30 max effort, standing start, on the minute". I've found that males tend to respond to the use of the word "you" as it implies an individual instruction.

Conversely, I've found females will respond to "you"; however, they seem better engaged when the word "we" is used instead. "We" is more of a group word and includes the coach, too, so you are part of the group. Of course, everyone knows the coach is not going to do the work, but it still demonstrates verbally that the coach is including themselves. Example: "We are going to run 4 x 30 max effort, standing start, on the minute". The interchangeability of the use of "you" and "we" when giving instruction sets is not mutually exclusive, nor "set in stone", however, it is worth considering the best pronoun/s to use when speaking to your athletes.

Mostly, I've had mixed groups. In those instances, I may explain the task twice, switching the "you" and "we" between explanations, and reinforcing that with eye contact with the sub-group I am addressing. Explaining an activity more than once may seem a waste of time, with the thought of "Why didn't they listen and understand the first time?" However, it is a better use of coaching time to explain twice and have the athlete perform correctly the first time.

Delivering Information

Not everyone receives information effectively the same way. Some athletes are visual dominant learners, some kinaesthetic dominant, some verbal dominant, with most having varying degrees of preference to each style of information presented. It is up to the coach to understand the preferred learning style of their athletes and deliver the information most effectively. This is where repeating instruction using different modalities of learning style will capture all your athletes.

Eye contact is crucial when engaging athletes. The athletes should also be looking at you when you are giving instructions, so make sure they are. The coach should always be cognisant of where the sun or flood lights are in relation to the athletes. It will be hard for athletes to concentrate if they are staring into the sun or flood lights, so move to keep the athletes comfortable to receive your message. In a larger group, ensure they can all see you and vice versa, and make eye contact with everyone. The visual feedback is an important indicator of how well your message has gotten through. It's better to spend a few moments longer to ensure everyone understands the instruction set than to have to pull up an athlete to re-transmit your instructions.

It is always worth asking if everyone understands what you have instructed. Invariably, everyone will nod in agreement that they understand, even if they don't. You could ask questions, but this can be fraught, as it may come across as singling out athletes whom you suspect of not knowing. This will potentially create a toxic environment very quickly, as the athletes will believe that you do not support them, and you may start losing their trust. It is much better to create a culture of openness, where an athlete can simply ask a question without fear or favour, knowing the question will be openly received and answered without prejudice. You should never think that a question from an athlete is "silly" or a result of them not listening, as it may be that you haven't been successful in conveying the information in the first place. I would rather repeat myself than have the athletes perform incorrectly and perhaps have that incorrect movement manifest itself.

I've mentioned this already, but it is worth repeating here. Having to repeat your instructions can be frustrating, but skip past that feeling and maintain emotional control. Remember, with juniors, you are most likely spending most of your time teaching and not coaching in its purest form.

Trust

What is trust in a coach/athlete context? The athlete has an explicit trust that you, as their coach, have their best interests at the core of the relationship. This includes being truthful and genuine in your communication.

I've heard numerous instances of coaches building up athletes' self-belief with false hope or "grey" information in the belief that this will provide a boost to the athlete's confidence and potential performance. There is no issue with bolstering an athlete's self-belief to perform; however, if that is based upon an too high elevated self belief based on current performance, or is just outright unachievable, what could the consequences be?

At best, the athlete believes they tried and didn't succeed this time. However, if they needed false hope to have self-belief, then that builds a poor foundation. More likely, is that the athlete's self-belief may suffer, that their trust and belief in you as their coach may diminish, it may make your task of lifting your athlete's confidence in future performances much harder, as you will need to re-establish the trust/truth relationship. In essence, providing unrealistic short-term performance goals delivered as absolutely achievable starts to erode the foundation of the coach/athlete trust relationship. It also may leave the athlete wondering if you really know them or have the knowledge to be their coach.

How much information to provide?

I am a believer in providing athletes from about the age of 12 with appropriate technical programming information. I do this to facilitate the engagement by the athlete into the understanding of the programming I provide, so they understand the purpose of the session and how it fits into the overall training cycle. A better engaged athlete provides a better "buy-in" into your program. For a newer coach, this can be a daunting prospect, but the more quality information you understand and can disseminate, the more confident you will become.

Using swimming as an example, this is the type of information I would provide to the younger (12-15 years) athletes as we go through the session program on the whiteboard. It must be borne in mind that the age group (12-15) has had minimal exposure to chemistry and human biology, so it is essential to keep it general, using minimal technical terms, and keep it easy to follow. Having said that, it is within reason to teach them, introduce technical terms and describe simply what the terms mean or how they would be expected to feel (emotionally and physically) during the session, using sensations such as: still can carry on a conversation at rest breaks; feeling slightly puffed; unable to talk; fatigue levels; feeling nauseous etc. Terms would include aerobic and lactate. If they know how they could be feeling during the session, then they become aware of their own emotional and physical reactions to the training set. This then allows the athlete to develop an understanding of emotional and physiological responses to various types of training, to self-monitor, as well as being able to read and understand the program on the whiteboard and be aware of what it is trying to achieve.

To run through two types of non-sport specific training sessions and how I would explain them to the athletes:

1. Aerobic: Take note of the distances we are covering, the number of reps/sets, and the short rest periods. I would ask them what they think the intensity level is (low). Ask them if they think low-intensity and relatively continuous sets are aerobic or anaerobic? The answer, of course, is aerobic, and depending on the age group, I would explain why we are doing this type of work, for how many weeks and what basic physiological changes we are trying to achieve. For example: increase in red blood cells to carry oxygen, increase cell energy manufacture (for the older athletes, maybe mention that it involves mitochondrial density) etc. Indicate that over the period, the programming will change slightly to increase in intensity week by week (until you move to aerobic threshold, then anaerobic work). Often athletes find aerobic work boring, particularly those who just want to sprint.

2. Anaerobic: Note how the distances have shortened from the previous aerobic work and the rest periods and intensity have both increased. Perhaps ask them, "Why?"

Allow them to ask questions. You can describe the physiological responses they may experience (as lactate levels dramatically increase, they may experience diminishing coordination, being puffed out, difficulty talking, and feeling unwell), as well as why the work is done.

The above simple examples provide a better engagement of your athletes in your program. I believe everyone works better if engaged, and for athletes, that engagement involves understanding the "why" of doing the prescribed work and how it fits into the season/yearly training plan.

Excellent communication is also essential in the area of skill acquisition. As a coach, you need to not only know the skill, but to be able to break it down into its component parts and know the correct sequence in the kinetic chain.

Young post-pubescent females

You should consider having a 'clinical' conversation (it's unnecessary to go into the biology) with post-pubescent females as a group on the topic of the potential for their cycle affecting their performance, in testing, training, skill acquisition and competition. This engagement is important as it lets the athletes concerned know that you are aware of the possible impacts their cycle may have on their performance and that you will provide support and understanding from a coach's perspective.

There are books and online resources available that delve further into the above to help you better understand the female hormonal cycle and athletic performance. I urge you to source at least a reliable but simply laid out book on this topic. I added the word "reliable" as there are more and more sources from poorly or ill-informed "influencers" to be found in this space. My online go-to suggestion would be the various national sports institutes as well as sport medicine online resources as a starting point, and don't just look at your own country's institutes, examples could include national institutes from Canada, UK, Australia as well as their sport specific and coach association websites (even from sports other than yours, as we're talking about generic information).

Other Coaches

This section is less about the actual communication with other coaches and more about recognising learning opportunities. It's always interesting to watch the interactions between coaches. Some coaches don't engage in any meaningful discussions with their peers, possibly because they don't want to give any "secrets" away. You've probably met the coach who believes that they have the key to success, which is, of course, a nonsense. You could have copies of Olympic-level coaches' training programs, but the likelihood of you producing the next Olympian within your program is quite remote. There is an array of inputs that go into producing an elite performer, with programming being just one.

The real development for you as a coach is to understand this array of inputs and learn how to implement them in a way that matches the developmental level of your athletes. Applying high-level athletic programming onto junior or new athletes will cause more harm than good, as they have not had the years of baseline development followed by associated controlled progressive development.

For your development, I would attempt to reach out to coaches who are open to mentoring a new coach. Ask a coach who is open to making themselves available if you can observe their training sessions from a distance. Also, ask them if they could spend a few minutes with you both before and after the session to provide information and answer any questions you may have to enhance your understanding of the "why".

New coaches often find they stay within the confines of their sport. For example, a football coach will spend time only within football, as does a netball coach, etc. Do you think that could be limiting your learning? Why would a coach want to spend time observing another sport?

The sports mentioned above (and there are many others) have a basic component in common. - being able to get moving quickly. This could be described as "first step quickness", or 2-5 metre acceleration. So if you coach in a sport that requires this initial quickness, why not spend time with a track sprints coach? After all, that's their "bread and butter"

Officials and Committees

Invariably, as a coach you will deal with officials, umpires, referees, judges, etc. Irrespective of what you think they have or haven't done, how justified or otherwise, they must always be treated with respect. Without them, there is no competition. They may be volunteers. They may make mistakes or errors. They are doing their best. Above all, your interactions with this group are being watched by parents/caregivers, and most importantly, by your athletes. You may think arguing with officials may be you standing up for your athletes, but it's not. It shows disrespect and sets a poor example for your athletes. It may be your athlete received a poor or incorrect call, but how often would you complain if the incorrect call favoured your athlete? Enough said on this. As a coach, you most likely have a code of conduct to abide to, so do so.

It may be that you are in a club environment, appointed by a club committee with a requirement to report regularly. Always furnish your reports on time, be concise, follow a consistent layout and don't embellish. The committee should also assist you by providing you with athlete/team selection guidelines or policies (if that's a part of your sport), as well as possibly managing issues with parents/caregivers. They can provide equipment through club funds as well as grant applications.

Unconscious Bias and Confirmation Bias

We all have biases we are aware of, which we try to temper and not have influence over our behaviour. However, we also have unconscious biases, which may be less obvious. As a coach, you need to be aware of your unconscious biases and ensure they do not interfere with your work.

They can be as simple as focusing on preferred athletes when addressing a group, or focusing on athletes you have formed a closer coach/athlete bond with during training, or talking more often to select parents/caregivers than others. The reasons may not be insidious but can be as a result of unconscious bias. There is no question that we are drawn to certain people more than to others, for any number of reasons. For example, you have your circle of friends, which precludes others. However, as a coach, this is not acceptable. I realise that's a bold statement however, you are a coach to all, and all deserve your time based on needs.

The above is something you need to be aware of, and regularly think back and review your training sessions and ensure equity of your time has been distributed to all over time. Obviously, at some point, an athlete may need more of your attention, but averaged over time, it should be relatively even.

How often do you see the same groups of people together, perhaps at the local cafe, in the school yard at pick-up time, coaches talking together? My guess would be quite often. Perhaps you do too. People cluster together for a variety of reasons, including similar interests, same thinking, personality etc.

As a coach, the notion of talking with other like-minded coaches or only reading articles that reinforce your thinking leaves you with a belief that you are right to the exclusion of any alternate thought. This is known as confirmation bias. Let's refer to it as how it's also known - "groupthink". How can "groupthink" improve your knowledge, when all you hear is the same message, which conforms to your current understanding or beliefs? As a coach, you need to be open to new ideas and perspectives. You also need to have critical thinking skills to be able to discern the validity of information presented to you, which, as a newer coach can be difficult.

There are numerous worthwhile in-person and online courses which I commend you to avail yourself of. The more time you spend understanding your own biases, the better placed you will be to become aware of them and manage them to become a better coach.

Motivation

The area of sports psychology is vast, covering many aspects of an athletes interpretation of the world as they see it, their response and their ability to perform.

> **Task:** What do you define as components of sports psychology? Do they vary depending upon which stage your athlete is in: sampling, specialising or investment years?

Instructional sports psychology is a fundamental component of coaching. It is defined as the coach providing instruction of motor skills/learning to the athlete. As a coach, you may have developed your instructional skills through past experiences, such as those with your former coach, education courses, readings in sport psychology, articles and books on motor learning. Although I cover this from one perspective in the 'motor skill acquisition' chapter, it's worth providing further information to broaden your understanding.

With this knowledge you can develop a systematic approach to instructional coaching, using the following proposed sequence:

1. A description of the competent performance of the movement desired, or the desired end result.

2. Assessment of the athletes current knowledge or ability before being given the instruction set (this will provide you with an athlete performance baseline against which to judge your instruction efficacy).

3. A learning phase.

4. Provision of instruction to transition the athlete to the desired endpoint after the learning phase.

5. Evaluate/assess the efficacy of your instructional coaching. This also involves including the athletes opinion of success based upon the instructional technique provided.

Instructional coaching for skill acquisition is broader than just a sequential step-by-step "flow chart". The above does not make allowances for the individuals psychological state. This chapter will provide information about two key components for your success as a coach – the athlete's motivation and the athlete's engagement.

As a coach, you are in a strong leadership position, especially with young athletes who are dependent upon you for both instruction and motivational support. Motivated athletes have confidence in their coach – but how can you achieve that?

> **Task:** What do you believe to be the competencies that you can provide to your athletes that are key motivators?

The majority of new/newer coaches coach junior athletes/teams. It is well documented that there is a high drop-out rate in this cohort when compared with an older cohort. The reason for the drop-out varies and can include time-consuming hobbies, friends influence, school commitments, emphasis on performance outcomes or a lack of motivation. The last reason has by far the greatest impact on ongoing participation and will be what this chapter will focus on, as it falls to a large extent within the sphere of influence of the coach.

Take a moment to think about why athletes take part in sport and remain engaged. It is imperative that coaches create a developmentally appropriate learning environment that encourages participation. Sometimes there is an emphasis on winning or constantly achieving improved PBs which is unrealistic, thereby focusing on results and not the process which can create an unsustainable and demotivating environment.

> **Task:** What does a quality coaching environment look like?

In a broad summary, there are 5 key motivators for junior athletes to participate in sport, all of which you as the coach can have control or influence over:

1. Perception of an athletes personal competence.

   Athletes are motivated to become competent, which in turn improves their level of mastery, which then creates a positive motivational feedback loop. The converse also holds, with a lack of movement towards mastery improvement creating a negative motivational loop.

2. Fun and enjoyment.

   This concept will vary between athletes and even vary between sports. For example, some athletes may find repetitive drills boring, while others may find them challenging.

3. Parents/caregivers.

   Coaches must develop a positive relationship with the junior athlete's parents/caregivers, as the parents/caregivers are a major source of motivation to the athlete, for example, by supporting the athlete's effort, teamwork, etc. Parents/caregivers can also be a source of demotivation, for example, by being overly competitive, emphasising winning above all else, etc.

4. Learning new skills.

This is inherently motivating as it creates both personal (but must be achievable) challenges for the athlete, as well as increasing competence (see point 1 above).

5. Friends and peers.

   Motivation includes working as a team as well as the social peer interactions created. As a caution, a coach who compares peer athletes is likely to undermine the motivation of all participants.

To develop motivated athletes takes both time and relationship building. As a coach, your behaviours can undermine the motivation of the athlete/team much faster than the time it takes to build a positively motivated environment. A coach's demotivating behaviours can be summarised in a list below:

1. Providing low levels of encouragement or support

2. Being controlling or authoritative

3. Promoting intra-team rivalries

4. Favouring the talented athlete

5. Punishing athletes for making errors

6. Creating a highly competitive training environment (in a non-elite training space)

7. Creating a "fear of failure" culture

As a coach, you need to understand the difference in the coaching environment you create when comparing junior athletes with more advanced/elite athletes. You should avoid emulating coach behaviour/environment exhibited within an elite structure, as it does not transfer 'down' successfully.

A positive motivational coaching environment is one where the coach exhibits behaviours that are reinforcing and encouraging, as well as providing a level of autonomy to the athletes, as opposed to an environment that is critical of performance.

It is worth reminding ourselves as coaches, that an athlete's perceived or real under-performance may be in part or whole attributed to our program or other intervention we have initiated.

Self-reflection of coach competencies – key athlete motivators

There are various theories of athlete motivation, some are variations of one another, others develop over time, some extend to managing higher level elite athletes including post-career, however as this book is focusing on non-elite athletes, I will focus purely on "Self-determination theory" (SDT). I believe that SDT can provide the coach with a valuable motivation playbook to assist them in determining how interactions affect motivation.

Motivated athletes have confidence in their coach. The importance of that statement should not be underestimated in your success. Your self-reflection and introspection as a sport coach can be distilled down to four key elements:

1. Motivational competency.

   Exhibited through the ability to influence the development of an athlete's mood and psychological skills. Motivational competency involves the coach being capable to develop positive thinking patterns that improve the athlete's abilities.

2. Game strategy.

The development, training, and implementation of game strategies that help the athlete to make good decisions. For non-game style sports such as track athletics and swimming, the game strategies are replaced with race strategies. These occur as a part of your design of deliberate practice.

3. Technique competency.

The coach's ability to instruct athletes and assess their abilities during training. For this, the coach requires an in-depth understanding of the movement pattern/s, being able to interpret any error/s and their precedents, and to provide verbal, visual, and/or kinaesthetic correction as required and as is appropriate for the individual athlete.

4. Character development.

This refers to the coach's ability to influence the personal development and positive attitudes of the athlete.

Of the above list, motivational competency has the least positive influence on an athlete's motivation. It still has a positive influence, but less than the other three competencies.

Earlier, I mentioned an athlete's autonomy as a positive motivator, but how does that come about, and how can a coach facilitate this development?

A role of the coach in athlete autonomy development is to facilitate the development of intrinsic motivation in the athlete. To help you understand this concept, I will expand on the self-determination theory as it relates to coaching.

Self-determination theory (SDT)

As coaches, we all want committed athletes. If you reflect on your own experiences, your and your peers continued participation in sport was facilitated by your positive motivation. There is an absolute relationship between athlete motivation and ongoing participation.

SDT is a valuable concept within the coaching framework to assist you in understanding how your actions, behaviours and language have either a positive or negative influence on your athlete's motivation. There exist two coaching styles within the SDT model: the controlling coach and the needs supportive coach.

The controlling coach refers to the coach who:

- uses intimidation
- controls the use of rewards
- exhibits excessive personal control
- uses negative conditioning
- focuses on the athletes behaviour
- operates within a tightly constrained structure (see definition further down)

The coach's controlling behaviours can lead to a transference of performance pressure (whether real, imaginary or self-induced) that the coach induces onto the athletes. These types of behaviours have a negative effect on athlete motivation.

As a new or even experienced coach, the performance pressure can be exerted onto the coach from club committees, parents, or athletes, and can be a common basis for the coach exhibiting more controlling and thereby demotivating behaviours. As a result, an often fundamental component that the coach uses to apply pressure on the athlete/team to perform is by focusing on results (an external element) and is therefore no longer process driven (an internal element).

An externally driven results-focused environment creates performance targets that have informative value; however, that can have a cascading negative motivational effect on the athlete/team.

An alternative is to establish a need-supportive coaching style with the goal of supporting an athlete's autonomous motivation and engagement. This style falls under the SDT umbrella.

Under the SDT model, athletes have three basic needs that should be fulfilled to become and remain motivated and engaged:

1. Autonomy

   - The coach offers meaningful choices.

   - The coach provides a rationale for decisions.

   - The coach supports athlete initiatives within the learning process.

2. Competence

   - The coach provides a structure that is process-oriented.

   - The coach provides information and feedback.

   - The coach provides consistency.

   - The coach creates a confident environment so that the athlete feels able to achieve the desired outcomes.

3. Relatedness

   - the coach is available to the athlete

- the coach shares genuine concern for the athlete's well-being by offering appropriate comfort and support when required

- the coach allows the athlete to develop both belief and experience within a caring environment

Providing a supportive environment can be challenging at times, and during these times the coach may fall into the role or persona of a controlling coach. As a controlling coach, the coach's actions will be seen as non-supportive, pressuring, damaging to the athlete input, and demotivating. As a coach, you may even start to contradict yourself about your expectations, causing frustration amongst your athletes. Further, your coaching output and efficacy may also be diminished through either a loss of athlete discipline or athlete burnout.

Employing an autonomy supportive coaching style may seem "soft" to some coaches, as it is most likely at odds with:

- How you were coached.

- You perceive 'elite' coaches to be controlling, so that must be the correct coaching style.

- You believe a controlling coaching style to be more effective.

- You believe that an autonomy supportive coaching style is too 'open' with no or unlimited boundaries or athlete constraints.

In some respects, the above may be true. However, if you implement both an autonomy supportive coaching style within a structured coaching program, you should end up with a positive outcome all round.

Athletes who are coached in a constrained or controlling coaching structure perceive a lower level of coach support and intrinsic motivation.

Definition: Constrained structure

Within a constrained or controlling structure the athlete feels obligated to remain engaged within the sport. This structure produces a controlled motivation driven by the athlete feeling that they are either externally or internally pressured or compelled to engage in the sport, or in a specific type of behaviour. It can be summed as the athlete experiencing an obligation of 'having' to be involved.

To summarise, a controlling coaching style leads to a maladapted perception by the athlete of 'having to', which leads to the athlete having difficulty in remaining engaged, and they are therefore more likely to drop out.

Conversely, when an athlete internalises their motivation (autonomous motivation), their willingness to participate is based upon their 'wanting to'.

There is evidence that a coach who provides a need supportive environment under the SDT model (autonomy support, competence support, relatedness support) will enhance the athlete's enthusiasm and commitment, which will be demonstrated by their increases in:

- Desire to perform well.

- Enjoyment.

- A greater value is placed on opportunities presented to them..

Self determination theory in practice

For an athlete, risk taking within a skill acquisition/learning environment is a critical component for achieving success. As a coach, from time to time, you will have some athletes who, in your view, underperform due to their worry about making mistakes, which in turn is a positive predictor of both mastery avoidance and performance goal avoidance.

Asking an athlete to take a risk is akin to asking the athlete to enter a space where the outcome is unpredictable and/or not within their locus of control, which can raise their level of anxiety to a performance interfering level. It also raises a risk/reward profile as well as the associated responsibility of outcome which the athlete and the coach must address beforehand.

Applying elements of SDT, an autonomy supportive environment provides a rationale for decisions/tasks, by:

1) Acknowledging (hearing and understanding) athletes' positive or negative feelings/emotions without judgement, which can:

   a) Build trust between the coach and athlete

   b) Assists in the athlete identifying and managing their emotional response, which is essential for improved performance development

   c) Creates an environment where the athlete becomes more comfortable in taking risks and learning

   d) Creates a safe environment for the athlete to be able to express themselves, which allows for more open communication between the athlete and their coach

e) Listening actively and validating the athlete's emotions (eg, by saying "It's OK to feel unhappy"), respond with genuine empathy, and use the interaction to teach them self-compassion (to treat themselves with the same compassion that they would exhibit to a team mate)

f) Be mindful of your emotional input, both verbal and non-verbal

2) Allowing independent coach supported training (only advised for more experienced athletes)

a) Increases the autonomy and self-reliance of the athlete

b) Increases the athlete's engagement by encouraging time management, goal setting, increased self-confidence, and motivation

c) Allows for coach-defined tailored programming as well as developing the athlete's skills to adapt without coach oversight

d) Must be carefully monitored and evaluated by the coach to ensure the training plan is adhered to in regards activities, volume, and intensity

e) With coach support, open communication, goal setting, and athlete education, the coach can provide scaffolding support around the athlete

f) Examples beyond direct skill, could include: strength and conditioning work; directed work using drills; mental skills work, such as visualisation

3) Avoiding controlling behaviours such as offering tangible rewards. (Tangible rewards are an extrinsic motivator,

shown to be ineffective over time, and do not fall within the scope of SDT.) Ideas of intrinsic motivators/rewards can include:

a) Allowing some independent training which can increase the athlete's sense of ownership

b) Setting the athlete's achievable goals and enhancing skill development, which can increase the athlete's overall belief in progress and improvement

c) Increase the athlete's feeling of belonging by acknowledging their fit and contribution to the overall team outcomes

d) Acknowledging both individual and team achievements which will reinforce the sense of accomplishment

e) Focus on the process of improving skills and technique over results

f) Develop a supportive and safe environment for all athletes

4) Encouraging friendships within the team/group should also be supported under the relatedness component, which builds connections with others and develops/enhances the quality of interpersonal relationships and group identity.

Task: How would an autonomy supportive environment look in your coaching practice?

Expanding the above four elements may provide an insight into how you can incorporate an autonomous supportive structure into your coaching.

Athletes experience a range of emotions, from the jubilation of winning/succeeding to the deflation of not succeeding. However, that can be a rather dichotomous view, by assuming there are only two opposites of emotion. There are a plethora of emotions exhibited between those two extremes; also, the same outcome can elicit a different emotional response from different athletes. It is also the case that some athletes are more analytical than emotional in their response, which is an equally valid response and does not indicate that they are not engaged.

The response from an athlete to the same circumstance will also develop and change over time. This can be due to

- Their developing emotional maturation level (particularly if they are juniors)

- Their developing ability to manage emotional control through experience and/or channelling techniques

- The changing/developing relationship between themselves and the coach

- Their maturation into the sport.

As a coach, you must develop an understanding of how each of your athletes responds, acknowledge that response, and also accept its validity.

Example 1:

At the end of a winning game, one of your athletes is 'jumping for joy', and another is showing only a mild response of elation. What do you perceive from these two quite disparate responses to the same outcome?

Both athletes are responding in a way appropriate to themselves. Perhaps one athlete operates on an outward emotional level and exhibits extroverted behaviours, while the other athlete may operate on an analytical level, separating emotion out. Neither response is right or wrong, they are their own valid, individual responses. As a coach you need to understand your athletes and be able to genuinely communicate with them in a way that validates their own feelings. This conforms with the SDT theory component of relatedness.

A coach should also understand the impact their emotional state has when communicating with their athletes. In the above example, the coach needs to be able to react in a genuine and comparative emotional manner as the athlete, so they are communicating at the same emotionally engaged level. This may mean the coach has to morph between differing states of excitement depending on who they are communicating with.

Genuine communication is an absolute, as athletes are quick to recognise disingenuous or condescending communication, be it verbal only (words and tone) or if there is a disconnect between what is said and the associated body language, which will not only be demotivating, but also erode the trust relationship between the athlete and coach.

A point worth considering when we are discussing the coach's emotional reaction and engagement is that the coach's reaction during a game/event can have a profound effect on each athlete's level of arousal. If for example, the coach is 'bouncing of the wall' with excitement after a score, what effect might that have on different athletes?

For some athletes, a hyper-excited coach (assuming this is not how they normally behave) may:

- Increase their arousal level much higher than desired so that it will affect their on-field/pool/court performance (a too high level of arousal may interfere with the athletes ability to make correct decisions, raise their anxiety level, interfere with their movement from a relaxed and efficient movement to inefficient and 'tight')

- Make no difference to their arousal level

- Reduce their level of arousal (less common) as it may be seen as disconnected from reality, or out of normal behaviour

- Increase the anxiety levels among the athletes as the change in the coach's behaviour may inform the athletes of the heightened importance of the score, adding to game/performance pressure

Example 2:

As a coach of new/newer athletes, it is likely that there will be new members joining the group at the start (or during) the season. The notions of relatedness and group acceptance are fundamental to the coach developing a cohesive and supportive coaching environment, devoid of toxic behaviours. There are various ways a coach can welcome new athletes to the group, the method of which can depend on the current group dynamics, the age of the group and the performance level of the group.

Examples of welcoming a new athlete to the group could include:

- Introducing them to the group with a short biography if appropriate

- Pairing the athlete up with a suitable partner who is non-judgemental, open, and welcoming

- Placing the athlete in an appropriate sub-group commensurate with their ability, so they don't feel overwhelmed

- Checking in on the athlete regularly

- Speaking to the athlete with a non-confrontational and encouraging manner (together with their parent/caregiver if they are there) about how they felt, if the session met their expectations, as well as how you see their performance.

Task: How can you encourage an athlete to take a risk? What defines a risk within a coaching environment?

Example 3:

I often encountered athletes who had a "risk of failure approach" to tasks, be it a new skill or a competitive performance (eg a game or a race). I found this to be more prevalent amongst early/mid adolescent than the younger or older athlete. What approach would you use to support the athlete in their performance attempt? My approach would be as follows:

- Fully understand the likely outcome of the attempt by knowing the athlete's potential at that point in time. In other words, as the coach you are realistic in your assessment of the likely outcome.

  If you overestimate the outcome by a sizeable margin you need to question your understanding of that athlete's performance ability at that time, or alternatively, you believe that if you verbalise that belief to the athlete that, it will motivate them to achieve. These are both demotivating behaviours that can lead to the athlete doubting your competence.

- Ensure you have developed a trust relationship with the athlete so that candid and realistic outcomes can be predicted, which in turn will reinforce both competence and relatedness within the SDT model.

- I have already mentioned the need to focus on process rather than outcomes/results, and this should remain the underlying rationale to help manage risk aversion and the athletes' often outcome/results focus. The outcome or result of a competitive performance is an absolute for all to see, but must be contextualised by the coach in discussion with the athlete. To do this, the coach should have a genuine understanding of that athlete's development as it relates to the outcome and where in the longer term process development the athlete is at. When brought together with performance statistics, a complete picture of realistic expectations can be negotiated. This will allow the coach and athlete to understand the individual nature of the athlete's development pathway as it relates to performance, and provide input into the process driven athlete development. This all forms part of the feedback loop back into the coach's programming.

- One method I employed with risk-averse athletes (or those who lacked confidence and self-belief to extend themselves), was to transfer the performance risk from the athlete to myself, thereby allowing the athlete to focus on the process of performance with the outcome of that performance resting purely with me. This was achieved through a developed trust relationship with the athlete, where they were instructed to focus on the performance, which may be to focus on only one performance element (eg lead early to the player with the ball), or to focus on individual consecutive performance elements throughout a single race (such as the start, stride length/stroke length, last ten metres, if running or swimming). During the post-performance review with the athlete, the discussion focused on the various process elements during the performance. The outcome is also discussed as a minor item within the overall process context. Obviously if the performance was higher than expected, then that should be acknowledged.

If the performance is well above expectations, then it could be that either the coach has underestimated the athlete's ability at that point in time, or the athlete has consolidated learning from deliberate practice, and together with a positive mindset, has been able to assemble a performance beyond expectation.

Conversely, if the performance process was not followed, or the outcome is well below your expectation (remember, outcomes are considered contextually by the coach), then that provides feedback into the efficacy of the coach's programming and it's delivery to that athlete.

Example 4:

There is an assumption that the coach will always be at a game or meet, but how would the athletes perform if the coach weren't there without prior notice? If the coach knows of their absence in advance they can inform the athletes in advance and put in an alternate coaching structure. There are several athlete responses to their coach being absent without notice, and they will vary between athletes, and could include:

- No tangible response at all – carry on as usual

- Raised anxiety level due to a lack of guidance and/or support

- Anxiety levels rise to a level of performance interference rendering the athlete unable to perform

The variance in possible responses can be put down to:

- An individual athlete's personality

- Self-confidence and self-belief

- Experience

- The level of coach reliance.

The level of coach reliance directly relates to the coach developing an athlete's autonomy within the SDT framework. The development of athlete autonomy requires the coach to relinquish their inherent coaching power over time, by allowing the coach-athlete relationship to develop towards a more egalitarian partnership. This does not imply that the coach is making themselves completely redundant, as they still develop the training programs and game day or race strategies, but within a coach/athlete collaborative environment.

To develop athlete autonomy within the framework, the coach educates the athlete in the reasoning behind the programming that the coach has developed, so the athlete gains an understanding of the science behind the program, and the coach, in return, achieves an athlete's 'buy-in'. Through this, the athlete also reinforces their belief in the coach's competence, which also serves to deepen the coach/athlete relationship.

Competence, autonomy, and relatedness are seen as social contexts, and if not supported in your coaching practice, will lead to a lowering of motivation and engagement and an associated decline in performance.

Movement Acquisition

To acquire movement (referred to as motor skill) requires the athlete to learn a new set of movements involving limbs or segments by coordinating the correct muscle groups via the neuromuscular system to create a movement to produce a desired outcome or action. It may also involve the senses, such as vision, hearing, and tactile feedback. Motor skill acquisition is acquired through motor learning.

This book will focus on the basic concepts of motor skills and motor learning.

Coaches often assess or teach movement as a whole, however we can divide motor skills into two categories: gross motor skills (for example, running, throwing, swimming) and fine motor skills requiring a high level of precision (for example, hand eye coordination), while many movements require a coordinated combination of both gross and fine motor skills.

The athlete is required to produce motor skills in either a closed, stable environment (for example, a free throw shot in basketball) or in a non-stable, open environment (for example, in an ongoing soccer game). Similar to teaching a complex skill by breaking down the skill into smaller teaching segments (or chunks), open skills are taught with initial instruction being in a closed environment with a progressive move towards an open environment. This can also be referred to as a teaching progression. For example, to teach batting to a softball/baseball athlete, a simple teaching progression may look like this:
1. hitting off a batting tee, ball height always the same

2. hitting off a batting tee, with varying ball height
3. hitting a moving pitch delivered predictably in speed and placement by a pitching machine
4. hitting a pitch delivered by a pitcher with varying speed and placement

Measurement of motor performance

We have already discussed outcomes versus processes, and at this point have probably concluded that we should focus our coaching attention and intervention on the process/segments that produce our desired action. That gives the coach a choice, a clear-cut distinction between outcome or process, but is it that simple?

Many sports can use the athlete's reaction time (RT) as a performance measure, that is, the time taken for the athlete to react to a stimulus and produce the required, correct movement.

> **TASK**: List instances where you could use RT.

Two examples could be: the RT of an athlete to a race starter's signal to commence the race (for example, at swimming or track) or secondly, the RT to initiate the correct movement dependent upon up-field or up-court movements (for example, in netball or hockey). These two examples are quite different, however, they each follow a similar structure which takes a measurable time:

Prepare for action : Generate a decision of how to react :
Produce the reaction/movement

With developmental athletes, the time taken to generate a decision and then to react to that decision (hopefully correctly) can seem quite long when compared to an experienced or elite athlete.

The above three-stage structure is compounded when a fourth element of "discrimination" is added to the mix. For example, in swimming or track, there is no discrimination in timing as there is only one solution to the starter's signal – to go! In field and court sports, there is a time based discrimination added due to the fact that there may be more than one signal to respond to. This is because up-field/up-court movements may be complex which in turn may impact the decision time as the athlete must discriminate between the signals received to determine which one is the more likely outcome/dangerous/opportunity within the field/court of play, which adds to the total response time of the athlete.

Consistency

There is one type of error that probably concerns coaches the most in the motor skill area - consistency. As a coach of new or newer athletes you would focus much of your time on consistency errors. As the name implies, it is when an athlete has an issue with successfully repeating a desired movement within an acceptable range of motion with consistency. If a lack of consistency occurs, then it would indicate that the athlete has not acquired the basic movement pattern needed for success. This can occur when the coach has ramped up the teaching too quickly or not given enough time for the athlete to consolidate the movement pattern along a progressive development timeline.

This is a common issue, especially for newer coaches in team sports, where it is difficult to deliver a coaching session that caters to all athletes and allows skill development time for a non-homogeneous cohort, as well as believing that they need to produce improvement along a linear curve to validate their coaching methodology. There is also the added issue for the newer coach in knowing when to observe each athlete and for how long, all the while ensuring an equity of their attention to all participants who are most likely developing their skills at different rates.

As you read on, you should start to understand the issues surrounding consistency errors and begin to gain an insight into their management as part of your coaching toolbox.

Motor control

As a coach, one of your key goals is to produce athletes with coordinated movement to a desired pattern. But what is coordination?

Coordination comprises two elements:
1. A pattern involving the head, eyes, body, and/or limb movements
2. The above pattern is produced relative to the environmental objects and events

Task: Take a moment before reading on to think about how the two points above could affect your skill teaching methods.

The teaching of a skill/movement is not normally taught in the context of a competitive environment; however, the coach does need to transition from a closed and controlled environment with tightly controlled variables towards the less environmentally controlled context of the competitive space. This is because the skill/movement taught in a closed environment may not naturally translate to the same performance ability once the constraints of the controlled environment are removed, potentially leading to a lower quality performance.

For example, catching a ball in a static environment with no opponent or game pressure/decision-making requirements may be repeated successfully; however, in a competitive situation, the athlete's performance may diminish in quality due to the change in environmental conditions.

Most competitive sport is performed in an open environment with other athletes and/or objects in motion, in other words, a dynamic space with changing variables. In these environments the athlete must interact with the competition environment by taking into account perception and movement variables to provide a decision framework from which they can make a determination of how to react. This is known as perception-action coupling, which is the coordinated coupling of visual perception of an object (or person) and the required limb movements to achieve the required action.

> **Task**: How would the perception-action coupling guide your coaching of both an athlete's movement development plan and athlete skill development in a game?

As a coach, you should plan effective instruction and practice environments as well as develop alternatives if the initial plans are not successful.

As a teaching point using motor control theories, when teaching a skill with a specific rhythm normally performed at a high speed, then in the first instance, the skill should be taught at a slow speed, with the speed increasing progressively only once the skill can be reliably performed at each incremental speed increase. The learning can be enhanced by segmenting the skill into logical, linked components and introducing these components with the use of drills.

The 'eyes' have it

Many sports require the athlete to run, be it on a track, court, or pitch/oval. Let's briefly touch on using motor control concepts to aid our teaching.

> **Task**: Do you think head stability when running is important, and if so, why?

When moving, it is a goal of the motor control system to maintain head stability, whether walking, running, or hopping/jumping. The brain receives sensory information from the environment via various means, including the eyes, as well as through proprioception, etc. In a game situation, the eyes may be tracking a ball in motion while the athlete is also moving. If the athlete's head does not maintain stability then the visual field is also not stable, resulting in the visual tracking of the object being less than optimal. For this reason, when teaching running in preparation for a field/court sport, head stability should be one of your teaching points.

> **Task**: One of the sports I played in my youth was baseball and I recall coaches always reminding players when batting to "keep their eye on the ball" inferring from the pitch to bat impact. This coach's line would be familiar to many in other sports too,

For all but the novice athlete, the above statement is not true. If it were true then a goalie in soccer would be unable to make a save, as they lose sight of the ball as it travels between players, similarly in ice hockey, as the puck travels in a non-high-lifted shot.

For catching a ball, research has shown that an experiences player needs to see the ball for only the first 300 milliseconds of flight to be able to judge its direction and distance, and again a similar time-frame before hand contact is made. The final visual data gathering by the athlete is to obtain time-to-contact information that will allow for the timing of the hand/finger coordination to complete the catch. That may be a minimum time needed for visual data gathering according to research, however normally the athlete would not view the ball in flight for these two short periods, but take short, regular visual samples to gauge the flight characteristics and make adjustments to their perception/decision in regards to the ball's flight characteristics, direction, distance and impact point. The flight path of the ball could be altered during flight by variables, including wind (speed, direction, turbulence) and ball spin (which could affect the rate of drop, curve).

As an aside, receiving visual information to facilitate the catching process of a ball/frisbee etc is only one element when coaching preadolescent and adolescent athletes, as many will experience growth spurts and some will take time to re-establish limb coordination as well as spatial awareness of where their limbs now end.

A key teaching instruction for the new or newer athlete is to watch the incoming ball for as long as possible during its flight to be able to better predict the impact point. Critically, the athlete should not watch to the point of impact (catch, trap, or hit), as that would require a head realignment, thereby changing the visual field, which would be counterproductive, as mentioned previously.

Another teaching point for catching, that is worth noting, is that less experienced athletes have a lower success rate if they cannot see their catching hand while attempting to make the catch. As experience grows, this visual feedback to see the catching hand becomes less until eventually is no longer required to ensure a successful catch. This notion links back to the athlete developing a spatial awareness of where their hand is in space and relating that position to the ball flight.

Decision time-frame

Competitive sport requires decision-making to elicit a physical response. For example, a defender will track the ball as it's in the opposition team's control as well as track player movements up-field/court (both opposition and own team) and track the player they are defending.

> **Task**: How much of an impact would the above have on an athlete's time required to decide of when, where and how to move?

Thinking about the above task, the impact on the athlete's RT would be quite high (RT = receiving all the stimuli, assessing each stimulus, and then deciding which would be the most likely valid prediction of future movement/game play, and then responding with the correct movement). There is a higher impact on RT with novice athletes due to their general inability to quickly discard irrelevant information and/or ignore irrelevant stimuli. Although the decisions occur relatively quickly (but may not be the correct decision) they still take time. But how long do they take?

If the athlete had only one choice, the reaction time would be in the order of 200-250 milliseconds (0.2-0.25 seconds). If the athlete has to make one of two choices, then the decision time extends to about 300 milliseconds. The time is a close guide only, as there are differences among individuals. If 5 choices are presented the RT extends to about 500 milliseconds. For readers who are interested in exploring this further, I refer you to Hicks formula, which is: choice RT $= k[\log_2 (n+1)]$, where 'k' is a constant (simple one choice RT) and 'n' is the number of choices.

So in essence, the more choices or inputs an athlete has as to their decision-based movement, the longer the decision-making process becomes before a reaction occurs. This concept probably sounds obvious and one we can all relate to. In the chapter on communication, it was identified that the athlete should only be listening to one voice – the coach's, to ensure the athlete follows cohesive direction. If we add a parent/caregiver/spectator on the sidelines calling out additional information, we can add choices to the Hicks formula and understand how the athlete's RT would be negatively affected. Athletes with more experience can usually block out the extraneous information from the sidelines, but new or newer athletes generally have difficulty in doing so. Other influences on increasing RT include:
- An increase in on-field/court movement complexity
- An increase in the accuracy required

- An opponent player 'faking' a move (you can gain further information on this topic by researching 'psychological refractory period')
- Reduction in alertness, fatigue, boredom, loss of motivation, not involved for extended periods (for example, outfield in softball; not having a ball come the athlete's way in cricket for an extended time)

Decreases in RT can come about through:
- Experience
- A repetition of movement within a discrete situation, for example, baseline rallies in tennis.
- If the athlete hears their name called out, it will spontaneously shift the athlete's attention to that verbal stimulus

To further reinforce the idea of "one voice", in a competitive situation, the coach's voice is meaningful, while sideline 'coaching' simply causes RT interference.

Attention capacity

As a coach to new or newer athletes in team sports, one thing you will most likely notice is that your athletes may not see what you may describe as "being obvious" on the field of play. But why can't your athletes see the obvious unfold or opportunities as they present?

A primary reason revolves around the brain having a limited capacity for attention. Expert athletes will limit their attention capacity to only relevant stimuli, thereby being able to make movement decisions more quickly, and with a greater accuracy of decision, whereas novice athletes will fixate their attention on more stimuli adding to their attention capacity load, leading towards a potential overload, slowing down the decision process and increasing RT, with a greater potential to action an incorrect decision.

To address the attention capacity limitation, inexperienced athletes will typically focus on only one or two primary targets, for example, in defence their focus will tend to be on the ball and the ball carrier which will limit RT interference, but limits their information gathering, whereas experienced athletes will focus instead on the positions and movement of players which allows them to infer where the play is moving.

Learning

You've most likely heard the oft-quoted saying "Practice makes perfect". I add a caveat to that, "you get what you practice", or to borrow a term used in computer programming: "garbage in – garbage out". My emphasis is this: you must fully understand and be able to explain, using different teaching modalities if needed, the movement/skill you are teaching and have a thorough knowledge of the movement/skill teaching progression.

When teaching a new skill using the correct teaching progression to an athlete, two things will stand out:
1. The athlete will improve quickly between attempts
2. There may be a large variance in the quality of the action/movement during the learning process from the beginning to the endpoint

During the first stage of an athlete learning a new skill, it is critical for the coach to observe and to provide augmented feedback often, to ensure an appropriate learning continuum/progression towards the correct movement.

Because this is a fundamental stage, it is also the stage where movement errors are not only prevalent but if not corrected, can manifest, potentially leading to the skill not being practised correctly with associated performance failure, leading to the need for movement deconstruction and the relearning of the skill and/or possible injury due to stresses on joints/segments moving in incorrect planes of motion, which can also lead to a potential for loss of motivation by the athlete.

Retention

As your athlete practices a skill, their ability to reliably perform that skill should improve over time. How can you determine how well they have learnt that skill?

Learning implies retention, so that after a period where that skill has not been rehearsed, the coach can assess the athlete's retention of that skill by having the athlete perform that skill. This may seem a little obscure, as surely skills taught are relevant to game play, etc, and are a regular part of the training program.

If an athlete has a break of several weeks or a longer inter-seasonal break, the quality of execution of a skill on resumption is indicative of their retention, and provides the coach with feedback as to:

- The athlete's retention
- The efficiency of the coach's teaching strategy
- The time needed for the skill to manifest
- Have sub-components of the skill been given enough time to become retained to allow the skill base to be built upon

If a skill has been retained and can be reliably reproduced even after a time lapse, then we can confidently say that the skill has persistence.

Once persistence has been attained, then the coach can expand the complexity of the skill, as the base skill/s have been learned. This is an important consideration when designing your program. If you're finding skill errors creeping in, then it may be that the skill's building blocks are not persistent, and you may need to go back a step.

A novel way to assess the learning of a skill is to have the athlete perform the skill several times with no augmented (verbal) feedback provided by the coach, so the athlete only uses their resources. The athlete should already be aware of the key teaching points during the learning process, such as movement sequence, joint angles, posture, as well as the feedback against their skin by the movement of air/water.

For a coach, this is quite important on two fronts:
1. To develop the athlete to become coach independent and thereby self-reliant and empowered for self-correction (which supports the SDT model)
2. To provide the coach with exact feedback as to where the teaching progression can be improved and where the athletes' movement information is deficient.

Another method of assessment of persistence is to alter the environment to place the athlete under stress, such as would be experienced in a competitive context.

Task: What environmental stressors would you introduce and why?

Examples of environmental stressors could be: adding a defender during basketball layup execution, or providing a game simulation experience. These provide the coach with an indication of how well the skill can be reliably transferred to a competitive environment.

Performance plateau

Whether an athlete is learning a skill or striving for performance outcome improvement, athletes often have their improvement stagnate for a time before further improvement occurs again. This is referred to as a performance plateau.

As a coach you need to be aware that an athlete's improvement in skill learning or outcome performance is not linear, but is a step-wise process, with an improvement gain followed by a plateau where no improvement is realised, before the next improvement step occurs.

This plateau stage is referred to as a consolidation or adaptation phase. This phase can occur due to the skill having distinct developmental stages, which are contingent on previous stage/s being consolidated before moving onto the next stage successfully, and can include:

- Loss of athlete motivation
- Athlete fatigue over a longer term (physical and/or emotional)
- The programming is not providing the correct stimulus to elicit the desired response (skill development, strength and conditioning, aerobic and/or anaerobic fitness, etc)
- Neural (building of neural networks) and/or muscular adaptation time requirements not being allowed for (together with the previous point). Note: this book will not examine neural networks or muscular adaptation in depth.

Programming skills

Task: When designing your practice session and you are introducing or extending a skill, when should this occur within your daily program and for what time duration?

An answer could be that skill work is taught at the start of the session and either performed to a set time allowance within the session, or until the skill can be produced, or the coach decides that an athlete's performance associated with the skill development is starting to decline and stops to avoid a negative outcome by practising incorrect movements.

As a coach, you may have concluded that skills are taught at the start of the session, but is that jumping ahead? In all likelihood, your new/newer athletes attend school during the day, so are at training after school. It is also a reasonable assumption that for athletes to learn a new/newer skill will require both physical and mental application, together with sound motivation and engagement. When initially greeting athletes, the coach should make an initial assessment of the athlete's readiness to participate in the designed session, in particular evaluating:

- Level of fatigue (posture and perceived level of happiness can be reasonable indicators)
- Ensuring appropriate hydration and nutrition during the day
- Motivation

These three simple noninvasive assessments, evaluated through a general "meet and greet," will help the coach determine if the planned session has a likelihood of achieving the outcomes planned for. The key takeaway is for the coach not to have their head buried in their phone or notebook, but to be engaged from the start for this assessment.

The next step would be the warm-up followed by the skills component of your planned session. The warm-up should reflect the skills components you are teaching in neural activation, joint and muscle warm-up. This should include building up to the desired speed of movement. The coach needs to be careful in their warm-up design so that the warm-up component of the session blends into the skill component in that it:

- Is appropriate to the planned session
- Provides enough neural activation and physiological warm-up
- Does not fatigue the athlete (neurally, emotionally, or physically)

I've mentioned "planning your session" several times in this section. Planning will be covered in more detail in a later chapter. Planning is critical to be successful as a coach. If you are not prepared for each session in advance but rather take an ad-hoc approach, you will be setting yourself up to fail your athletes.

The duration of practising/learning a new skill has two main components for the coach to consider:

1. A more complex skill will be logically broken down into sub-skills and then progressively assembled into a contiguous movement
2. When athletes are exposed to a new skill then fatigue levels will increase at a higher than expected rate, due to:
    i. the high level of conscious attention being applied to a new skill

ii. higher energy cost associated with movement due to a lower economy of movement and less efficiency (both mechanical and physiologic efficiency)

Within the athlete's skill acquisition there are three kinematic goals to achieve: displacement, velocity and acceleration. The coach should also be aware that the kinematic elements do not develop simultaneously.

The first of the kinematics to develop with a new skill is displacement, and this should be the coach's initial teaching focus. (Displacement refers to the spatial characteristics of a skill – the three dimensional location points in space) After displacement, the velocity of movement becomes the focus and then the acceleration components.

As the athlete practices a new skill and their proficiency increases, the amount of conscious attention that they focus on the skill execution diminishes over time, allowing the skill to appear automatic in execution. This, in turn, frees up the athlete's limited conscious attention to be applied elsewhere.

As an example of the above, if the athlete attempts a relatively new skill during a competitive scenario, the skill may appear 'clunky' or the coach will notice that the athlete has not noticed changes in the dynamic field of play. This demonstrates the concept of dynamic attention availability and to what the athlete applies it. More experienced athletes will be able to execute the skill and be able to see and respond to changes in the field of play, because of their ability to assign conscious attention away from the skill execution, which for them is now "automatic".

Teaching skills

It is logical that the coach not only designs the teaching of broad skills from the basic to the complex, but also has the individual skill components sequentially broken down into the basic single segment movements before progressing to a more complex multi-segment movement.

The questions the coach needs to answer include:
1. What are the basic, broad foundation skills of the movement that need to be learned first?
2. What are the precedent elements? (You need to be able to walk before you can run concept)
3. What is the logical movement development progression of the skill?
4. What are the key focal teaching points for each element?

The coach needs to decide when each component is introduced and how that will impact or set the foundation for skill components further along the teaching progression to be built upon. This may seem easy, but it does require thought to ensure each element is built on the preceding element with no learning gaps, and importantly, enough time allowed for the elements to be reproduced, but not too long a time for the athlete to feel they are not being challenged with new learning and thereby losing motivation. This is particularly challenging for the coach with a non-homogeneous group (which is most likely), to ensure that all the individual skill levels are attended to, and all athletes continue to develop their skills at a rate applicable to them.

I've seen cases where coaches either bring the group down to the lowest common denominator of performance and program only in that space, or conversely, spend much less time than needed with the struggling athlete while preferring to focus on the 'high' achieving athletes. Both of these scenarios are unacceptable. Coaching groups is not easy, and all athletes should receive the attention and care required to enable them to grow within the sport. The ability of a coach to recognise individual needs and address those needs within a group of varying abilities takes a lot of effort and application.

Feedback in learning

Task: Do you think a demonstration is always the most effective method of instruction?

As a coach, you've decided that a visual demonstration, would be the most appropriate method to teach a particular skill. After the demonstration you ask your athletes what they saw, and behold, you get different answers. How can that be? Didn't they all see the same demonstration?

You need to ask yourself:
- Did all the athletes have the same perspective of the demonstration, or were athletes at different viewing angles and distances away? That would give them different physical and environmental reference points.
- Were the athletes aware of the key skill focus points or did you leave it up to them to determine that?
- Although athletes were all looking at a demonstration, what were they as individuals seeing? 'Looking at' and 'seeing' are very different.

When an athlete gathers visual movement information from an observation, the athlete determines reference points to generate a movement pattern, and then assembles that pattern and invariant reference points into a reproducible action based on patterns of the observed movement.

With that in mind, it is self-evident that athletes should observe a skill being performed expertly during the teaching process, as that generated movement pattern derived from perceptions should resemble the 'expert' as closely as possible. It is also important that the skill/movement is performed expertly several times before the athlete attempts a replication. However, most of the time, the athlete is likely to be observing a fellow novice athlete attempt to perform the movement as they wait their turn.

Task: Do you think that an athlete learning a new skill/movement would perform better or worse by observing their fellow athlete's attempts?

It may come as a surprise, but it can aid their performance development through the following means:
1. Observation of other athlete' attempts and mapping the observed movement against their own perception
2. Taking the above-gained comparative information and overlaying that with the coach's feedback to the other athletes to modify their movement image
3. The athlete observes/hears numerous instances of coach feedback to other athletes as well as more expert skill/movement demonstrations performed by the coach/expert as part of the feedback

The last part of the third point is very important, as the more frequent expert demonstrations the athlete observes, the better the skill/movement learning. The ongoing demonstrations during practice aid learning.

What if the skill/movement is rhythmical? Would a visual observation suffice? Yes, it could, but the learning process would be less effective. For example, teaching the correct speed of movement of the kick in butterfly to allow a seamless integration into the whole stroke development later, a visual observation provides the movement pattern, but if the coach also provides an audible cue such as clapping their hands to the required timing speed, then the athlete will have a better learning outcome through more successfully aligning the timing speed with the movement.

Verbal instruction

Coaches tend to explain, and explain and explain. As you will recall, we have already broached the notion of a person's limited capacity for information attention.

Bearing the idea of limited capacity for information attention in mind, instructions should be limited to only one or two elements, so the coach needs to have a solid understanding of what they want to have achieved (in learning or correction) and have the succinct language to achieve it.

Task: What should your verbal instruction focus on: the actual movement pattern or the movement outcome?

There is evidence that the feedback instructions should focus on the movement outcomes and less (or not at all) on the actual movement pattern itself. Although this is the case, with new/newer athletes being taught the initial skill/movement, it is important to allow the movement pattern to be understood and recognised, which is part of the 'art of coaching' – the knowing of when to apply which strategy.

For athletes who are past the very basic initial pattern recognition stage, focusing on movement outcomes could be more productive to elicit change as well as persistence. Focusing your verbal instructions/feedback on movement outcomes allows the athlete to engage in discovery learning.

Discovery learning allows the athlete to practice the skill with the action goal in mind and to discover how to achieve the action goal. Within this concept, the coach is almost in the background, allowing the athlete to go through the discovery process with minimal guidance.

Irrespective of the sport, athletes at various times need to move a segment/limbs with both accuracy and speed.

> **Task**: As a coach, you recognise the need for both accuracy of movement and speed of movement, but which do you emphasise first and why, or can they be taught simultaneously?

Accuracy is discussed here as the accuracy of movement of segments/limbs with accurate environmental interaction (as examples: hand entry in swimming or foot placement for high jump take-off).

Coaching literature is very clear that the emphasis should be on accuracy of movement and not speed of movement. If the coach emphasises speed over accuracy of movement, then the accuracy of movement will deteriorate. If a coach emphasises both speed and accuracy, athletes tend to focus on the speed component of the movement at the expense of the accuracy, with the resultant loss of accuracy of movement.

The notion of repetition of movement is important during the learning process, as long as the repetitions are improving over time in their correctness. As part of the coach's responsibility, the coach cannot allow repeated errors of a movement pattern to be repeated without intervention (augmented feedback) to avoid the incorrect movement pattern from manifesting with the athlete. This represents one of the challenges in coaching a group, as the coach needs to be vigilant over the entire group and not just focus on a subset. The coach needs to develop their skills in being able to quickly review and intervene (including providing positive feedback) by ensuring that they have an absolute knowledge of both the parts of a movement as well as the movement pattern in its entirety, together with an intervention toolbox to draw upon to be able to individualise the feedback for each athlete.

It has already been suggested that coaches can over-explain to the athlete, bombarding them with reasons, instructions, rules etc and the effect that has on the athlete's limited capacity of attention. To help address this, coaches should use verbal cues in preference to verbose descriptions.

Verbal cues are short, discrete phrases limited to a few words in length that direct the attention of the athlete to specific skill performance components, which could relate to the field of play

focus or a movement skill-specific focus, eg, "more body roll', '
lift your knee higher', 'look at the ball'.

When providing verbal cue information to the athlete, the coach
can ensure a greater success by including a relevant demonstration
that mirrors or reinforces the verbal cue. For example:
- A swim coach may say "more body roll" and accompany
  that with a demonstration of how much shoulder and hip
  rotation is being asked for
- A coach may ask for the hips to remain along the vertical
  body line when running as opposed to the hips being
  behind the vertical body line, with a demonstration
  (usually over-emphasised) of each posture.

The coach can also provide the athlete with their cues to focus
attention on specific elements of the movement. These become an
athlete's prompts to aid in the execution of the performance and
skill persistence by becoming a step-wise vocabulary. These
prompts are not complex, but are normally just one word. For
example, four prompts for a basketball free throw may be:
- 'feet' – align feet square to the line
- 'balance' – ensure proper weight distribution
- 'ball' – hold the ball correctly
- 'basket' – sight the target

A key for the coach to bear in mind is that the verbal feedback
needs to be consistent in language. If the coach regularly alters the
words used for the same verbal feedback item, then the athletes
will have difficulty associating the verbal cues with the
movement/correction, thereby diminishing the feedback efficacy.
That is not to say the coach cannot change the words used to
describe the cues to be more effective as they learn the best

communication language (or to individualise communication to meet an athlete's needs), but to avoid language change in an ad-hoc manner, every time the same thing is explained. As a coach, you need to be 'language flexible', for example, when you are teaching or correcting a movement to an eight-year-old the language used is most likely going to be different when the same explanation is given to a fifteen-year-old. Similarly, there will most likely be a difference in the words/language the coach uses when talking to a novice athlete as compared to an experienced athlete.

Augmented feedback

Your athlete already receives intrinsic (internal, self-directed) feedback when performing a skill. Depending upon the environment, this could include visual, auditory, proprioceptive, and tactile. The athlete's internalised feedback is then supplemented by augmented feedback, which has two components:
1. Knowledge of results (KR)
2. Knowledge of performance (KP)

At first glance, KR seems self-explanatory. For example, has the athlete delivered the arrow into the bullseye in archery, what time has the athlete achieved, etc.

KP refers to the information available about the athlete's movements that resulted in the performance goal. Reflecting on the definitions of KR and KP, it becomes clear that as a coach, the focus should be on KP, which then provides the basis for augmented feedback to the athlete.

Augmented feedback serves two purposes:

1. It provides information to the athlete about how they performed the skill and/or the skill performance development immediately, or as close as is practicable to the performance delivery.

2. It forms the basis for motivation of the athlete, as it can reinforce incremental improvements in skill performance over time.

Task: Do you think augmented feedback of KP should always be provided? If not, why, and when is it not required?

If the athlete cannot access intrinsic feedback, or alternatively if they are a new/newer athlete to the skill they may not have the tools/experience to utilise intrinsic feedback, then augmented feedback becomes an important element of developing the skill.

An example would be when an inexperienced athlete (in the skill) receives intrinsic feedback, eg, joint angles, but due to the lack of experience or KP cannot interpret the information, so requires the supplementation of augmented feedback.

Augmented feedback related to movement has a particular impact when the movement involves a coordinated multi-limb movement pattern. The feedback provides corrective information to the athlete, allowing the athlete to 're-map' the movement pattern, which in turn can provide them with intrinsic feedback that they can then apply.

Previously in this chapter, I spoke of athletes being able to improve their movement performance by observing other athletes together with hearing the coach's feedback on those attempts, so it raises the question, is augmented feedback that essential, or can it interfere with the athlete's learning?

As a coach, you also need to be cognisant of always providing augmented feedback on every attempt, as the athlete may develop a dependency on that feedback to be able to produce the skill/movement. The result of the athlete becoming dependent upon the augmented feedback may lead to a deterioration of performance.

Feedback to the athlete is covered by one of two themes:
1. Error correction of performance correctness. If the focus is completely on skill/movement error correction, the athlete may get the sense that they are not achieving any performance improvement, which has a demotivating influence. This is an area coaches can fall into as they strive to have their athletes succeed.
2. The alternate is for the coach to focus heavily on what the athlete is doing correctly. Focusing on the positives tends to ignore the errors and can give the athlete a sense of higher achievement than is delivered, however; the athlete may feel more motivated through their self-belief in their performance ability.

As a coach, you want your athletes to improve and to be motivated at the same time, so you need to provide both error correction and performance correctness feedback. The questions then arise:
1. At what point to provide the feedback?
2. How much feedback of each type to provide?
3. Is there a preference as to feedback type depending on the athlete's skill level?

Either type of feedback should not be provided to the athlete during skill/movement execution, to allow the athlete to fully focus on the intrinsic feedback they receive during the skill/movement execution. After the skill/movement execution, I would normally ask the athlete how the skill/movement execution felt to them. This is invaluable information, as it provides the intrinsic information gathered by the athlete as feedback which assists the coach in formulating their feedback to the athlete by incorporating a specific element or two into a more general statement, which both validates and values the athlete's feedback which can be highly motivating.

How much and what type of feedback to provide is guided by two factors:
1. What level of mastery the athlete exhibits
2. What are the skill foundations already in place

Generally, the newer the skill is for the athlete, the more the feedback focuses on error correction. This makes sense, because as a coach, it is incumbent on you to develop skills in the athlete along a progressive teaching pathway, with no introduction of skill/movement errors.

A consideration for the coach during this phase is to maintain the athlete's motivation, because to the athlete, it can feel that they are only receiving error corrective feedback which can be construed as being negative. The coach must also be mindful of not providing too much feedback, as has been previously discussed.

Once the foundation movement patterns are in place, the coaching focus becomes more on refinement of movement, so the feedback leans more towards overall performance correctness.

In conclusion, the feedback provided to correct errors will improve skill acquisition and feedback highlighting correct performance will improve athlete motivation, so ideally the coach would provide a thought-out blend of the two feedback types, the proportions of which vary depending on the feedback goals.

Having discussed the basics of error correction feedback, we can review its application based on the coach's view of the movement pattern. As a coach, you should have a visualisation of what the movement (segment or multi-segments) should ideally look like, and you base your feedback to the athlete according to an overlay of that movement. A key question to ask is how far removed from the 'ideal' movement (known as degrees of freedom) you allow before intervention is provided? The degrees of freedom of movement that the coach allows are referred to as the scope of movement.

Once the coach has determined that the movement is outside the scope, they need to formulate their feedback. To assist in this formulation, the coach would look at the kinetic chain of movement and derive a list from the most critical to the least critical errors. This is not the same as assigning importance to movement elements, but rather which movement element is the most critical (the most contingent) to performing the skill.

The most critical element should be the focus of the coach's feedback. For novice athletes, the feedback should include two components:

1. Identifying and describing the error (being mindful of not overloading the athlete with information), as well as correction information – in other words, a diagnosis followed by a prescription.
2. If the athlete is more advanced in the skill/movement development, then identifying and describing the error is usually enough.

As a coach, we understand that the provision of feedback is a critical component to athlete success, as is the type of feedback. However, the feedback type is only one component, with the frequency of feedback also needing consideration.

Feedback after each attempt has already been discussed, highlighting the athlete's limited capacity of attention, producing a diminishing return due to the cumulative effect of repeated feedback on each attempt. To counter this, the coach could provide feedback less often, thereby reducing the impact on the limited capacity of attention and allowing the athlete to self-correct on some attempts, which allows for an experiential self-discovery learning technique.

When feedback is provided less often, there is less likelihood that the athlete will develop a reliance on the feedback always being available, which is more realistic in a competitive context and assists in developing athlete autonomy.

Practice environment

In coaching, we've all experienced an athlete perform a skill/movement perfectly at practice, only to be unable to reproduce/transfer the skill/movement into a competitive environment.

Task: What do you think could be the cause and also the solution of the above issue?

Generally, coaches of field/court sports provide the athletes with a very consistent practice space and routine. While it may seem sound coaching practice to control all variables and keep consistent activity parameters, it has been shown that by creating a variable space results in better learning outcomes.

There are a host of variables that can be altered, for example:
- Indoor/outdoor
- Taking a free shot at the goal in the last moment of practice to win
- Changing the distance for shots from the standard spot
- Audio interference (crowd noise, music, etc)

The notion of organising a variable practice environment to aid learning should not be overlooked. Coaches normally use the same script, week in - week out, year in – year out, when teaching skill/movement in an attempt to establish persistence, only to find that in the variable competitive environment, the athletes struggle to reproduce the skill/movement to the same level as at practice. Often the coach apportions the reason for under-performance to 'competitive pressures'.

A drop in performance expectation may be partially due to competitive pressure; however, it may also be due to the athlete not being exposed to environmental variability, creating a positive interference effect on the learning outcomes.

The coach should be mindful when designing and delivering skill development, to determine how closely does the learning environment reflect the competitive environment. This concept forms the basis of 'specificity of practice'.

Whole skill, or part skill?

When teaching or refining a skill, the coach needs to decide whether the skill/movement can be taught as one contiguous action, or if it would be more successful if the skill/movement was taught in segments and then assembled.

A skill/movement in sport usually involves multi-segment movement/timing or other complexity, with coaches tending to reduce the complexity of the skill/movement by simplifying the overall skill/movement requirements by breaking it down into segments. Segmentation of complex skill/movement also reduces the attention load on the athlete.

This can also be referred to as a 'task teaching' (or 'micro-tasks) progression, when the athlete can either progress from:
- Easy to more complex
- Environmentally stable to variable
- Segments taught with the use of drills, which are then assembled into a contiguous, correctly timed movement pattern.
- Slow speed progressing to the required speed of movement while ensuring the correctness of movement within the desired range of that movement

If the coach determines that a whole of task is the most effective teaching modality to utilise, then the coach needs to determine what element of the whole movement the athlete should focus on, while the coach observes the movement as a whole. If the coach notices more than one error within the movement (out of scope, timing error etc) then it may be appropriate for the coach to reconsider and change to a progressive segmented teaching modality.

The challenge for the coach when using a segmented modality is to ensure no errors in skill/movement patterns or timing are introduced upon reassembling the skill/movement as a whole. To prevent errors from coming in, the coach needs to have a solid knowledge of the skill/movement and to understand the 'natural' break points that occur within that skill/movement to enable the separation into distinct, cohesive and sensible learning elements.

Depending on the skill/movement being taught, a progressive teaching model could involve:

- Teaching a very basic version of the whole skill/movement and then progressively adding increases in complexity as the whole skill/movement develops
- An initial movement segment is taught at a basic level, then the next basic movement segment is added on, and so on, until the whole skill/movement is realised as a compounding type model. Then the whole skill/movement is progressed in complexity
- Using a drill to lead into an action (eg, fast foot ladders leading into a short sprint)

The coach also needs to keep in mind the individual learning style or requirements of each athlete to maximise the quality of their learning time. This requires forethought and planning at an individual athlete level.

Skill acquisition is very complex, as the coach is teaching a group of people who have a range of individual needs, backgrounds, and innate abilities, all at the same time. This chapter has given the new/newer coach a broad overview of providing a teaching environment for their athletes. I have deliberately not included areas of brain function or neural network development in this book, as it's out of scope at the early coaching stage. I urge any coach who wishes to broaden their understanding to do further reading and research in this area. A greater applied knowledge will only improve your efficacy as a coach.

Evaluation of Skill Acquisition

If I mention "skill acquisition", what do you think of? Perhaps transferring the knowledge that you have of a skill to an athlete, or possibly teaching the athlete a particular movement or game play. To enable this to occur, you must develop that knowledge of the movement/skill and then use that knowledge to develop an observational model of evaluation, allowing you to make appropriate interventions to improve performance.

A cornerstone of skill acquisition and motor learning is for the coach to be able to utilise an observational model of evaluation

What is performance measuring?

In its most obvious form, performance measuring concerns both the quantitative and qualitative measurement of movement in isolation, or the results of that movement performance in competition. The data collected is then turned into information, which is then fed back into your coaching program to gauge the effectiveness of the stimulus you have provided, and also to highlights areas where your stimulus has been ineffective in showing improvement or new areas where improvement can be made.

Notice in the above paragraph, I am referring to the stimulus that you have provided. With that thought in mind, are you measuring an athlete's performance to support your testing regime, or are you testing to provide comparative information on the athlete's development? In other words, are you measuring performance because you think you need to as a coach, because you believe your athletes expect it, or are you testing as a feedback mechanism back into your programming? This is fundamental to the motivation behind the reasoning of why you are measuring performance in the first place. Remember, it's the effectiveness of the intervention/stimulus of your programming design and your athlete's response to that programming that you are measuring.

Please note, I will not be covering the statistical application and interpretation of your collected data, as it's outside the scope of this book. There are excellent texts available dealing with this topic.

My motivation for testing performance is that it reflects the efficacy of my programming of the development of the athletes, not because it's "what coaches do" or because athletes expect it. The results provide a feedback loop back into my programming.

Testing can also have the added benefit of exposing athletes to performance pressure within a supported training situation. As a coach, it is difficult to simulate the exact pressure of competition, but testing, or internal games/trials can go some way towards that simulation. It is also worth noting that testing and/or game simulation work also allows you, the coach, to appreciate how your athletes cope with both performance and decision-making under pressure, however, it can never really reach the pressure levels of an actual meaningful game.

Introduction to using qualitative bio-mechanical analysis to improve technique

From a basic coaching perspective, bio-mechanics encompasses the area of study concerned with the effect of forces on an athletes musculoskeletal structures. In reality, bio-mechanics covers much more, but we will focus on this definition and how it can help us in our coaching. Bio-mechanics tends to be associated with elite athlete management, however, as a coach, you can also collect and interpret this type of data using simple tools, such as a stopwatch, measuring tape, video etc.

For our discussion, bio-mechanical analysis serves two goals:
1. The primary goal is to improve performance
2. The secondary goal is to prevent injury

Describing movement.

As a coach, you not only need to have a theoretical understanding of the movement, you also need to be able to describe what the most effective technique would look like.

> **Task**: Pick a performance from your chosen sport (eg, one complete running cycle from right foot ground impact to the next right foot ground impact, or a swimming stroke cycle, or a softball pitch, etc) and write a step-by-step description of the movement.

Once the ideal movement has been described, the coach can then determine which movement elements performed by the athlete are correct or incorrect, effective or ineffective, safe or risk injury, etc. To assist the coach in making determinations to improve technique, the following elements are considered:

- Describe the ideal movement/technique. This will allow the coach to compare the observed movement with their concept of the ideal movement.
- Know the rules within the sport governing the movement. Rules impose constraints on the athlete of what they can and can't do.
- What is the athlete trying to achieve? The answer to this question is usually easy to answer, as it mostly involves goals: higher, faster, outmanoeuvre etc. From that end point the coach then translates the goals backwards into movements to achieve the goals as precisely as possible.
- Determine the most effective movement technique. This can be done by the coach observing high performance athletes perform the skill/movement and then determining what the various segments/elements that are positively contributing to the result. A note of caution must be included here: high-performance athletes may have unique elements to their movement that have been tailored just for them, possibly due to a unique physiological difference they possess.

Another way to determine the most effective movement is by reviewing the coaching and teaching literature and determining what each element contributes to the skill/movement.

When performing this breakdown, new/newer coaches can sometimes become fixated on limb movements, but they should also use elements such as the athlete's centre of gravity, rotational speed and timing, eye movement, and focus, etc, in determining their effective model.

Error evaluation

The first item in this process is to identify the error correctly, within our pre-determined degrees of freedom.

Although an athlete's movement may not reflect the ideal image/pattern in the coach's minds eye, the questions to ask during the error identification process are:
1. Is it only an individual style difference that doesn't detract from the movement's goal, or does it impact on the movement's goal?
2. Does the athlete have morphological differences from the 'ideal' athlete in the coach's comparative model (eg height, weight, strength, flexibility)?

The next step is to evaluate the error.

As a coach, the prevailing thinking is often "I must always correct movement errors, that's what coaching is". But is that thinking correct in all circumstances?

There are several key considerations the coach should think about to help guide them in their intervention, or if indeed intervention is needed.
• Does the perceived/identified error impact the performance outcome?
• Is the coach seeing the outcome of the error, or are they seeing the actual skill/movement error? In other words, is the error the coach 'sees' the result of a previous skill/movement error further back along the chain of movement?

- Is the error correction as simple as providing corrective instruction, which may result in a 'quick fix', or does it require a re-engineering of the skill/movement, which may take a medium time frame, or lastly, is the error caused by a strength or flexibility deficiency, which may take longer to correct?
- Critically does the error have the potential to cause injury to the athlete?
- Is the movement within the rules of the sport?

A final point to consider during the error evaluation process is to keep in mind the stage the athlete is at in their skill/movement acquisition. For new/newer athletes the evaluation should focus on the correctness of the coarse skill/movement components, whereas for a more advanced athlete, the evaluation focuses more on the finer skill/movement elements.

The bio-mechanics section has been deliberately kept short to remain within the predefined concept of keeping the book at a basic level. If you wish to deepen your knowledge, then I suggest you either enrol into physiology and bio-mechanics University coursework, or study texts in you own time. Broadly, information should at a minimum cover: skeletal and muscular structures with their associated interactions and stresses, force generation and management, and the physics of linear and rotational movement.

Qualitative evaluation.

Qualitative evaluation is an observational model for capturing bio-mechanical movement and assessing whether the movement is within an acceptable range of motion. In other words, you are observing and assessing the quality of the movement. Qualitative data can be collected and converted into numbers for data analysis, but that is outside the scope of this book. I will however, go through the process of capturing the movement, potential pitfalls, and how to incorporate the information into your coaching.

In its simplest form, qualitative testing can be defined as how an athlete moves through your visual field is interpreted against what you believe to be the ideal movement pattern or range of movement. Qualitative athletic evaluation is by far the most complex, as what you believe appears to be within the scope of an acceptable movement, to another coach it may not. The evaluation of the movement is also perspective-dependant with potentially numerous visual data points requiring collective assessment, but more of that later.

It is also worth pointing out that sometimes a qualitative evaluation will lead to a quantitative evaluation to confirm where an issue may be (quantitative evaluation is discussed later in this chapter). For example, I noticed one of my newer athletes had difficulty with ankle dorsi-flexion (bringing toes towards the shin). I got him to perform a squat to see how far he could squat before his heels left the ground (still in the qualitative area). From that, I decided to get out my Goniometer to measure ankle flexion (a device with two linear arms, one fixed, the other moves about a 'protractor" to yield a degree of movement angle result). This gave me a quantitative assessment of degrees of flexion, so over time I could accurately assess progress in flexion improvement.

There are 4 guiding components to follow when establishing a qualitative assessment:
1. Knowledge

a) of the activity you are assessing
b) of the critical features of the movement
c) of the goal of the movement
d) of the athlete (to allow for individual differences)
2. Observation
    a) you have identified the best vantage points to conduct the observation from
    b) you have identified the number of observations required
    c) you have identified the length of time for each observation
3. Evaluation
    a) identify the range of degrees of freedom allowed for of the critical features of the movement
    b) understand the kinetic chain of the movement to determine the movement sequence
    c) identify the error/s of the movement
4. Intervention
    a) select appropriate interventions, such as: verbal and visual feedback, modification of the task, mechanical guidance, and drills
    b) translate the identified critical features into cues for the athlete

Your observation of athletic performance must be planned so you can create a systematic observation strategy that is relevant to the movement/s you are planning to observe. Key components of a systematic observation strategy would include:
- Knowledge of the movement to be observed
- From where is best to observe the movement
- Acceptable range of movement (degrees of freedom)

- Critical features of the movement that make up an observation table
- Individual athlete differences
- Recording

Knowledge of the movement

Over the years, I've asked coaches what may be seen as almost inane questions, such as in softball – "how do you throw a ball?" I've had answers come back along the line of "well, like that," accompanied by a short demonstration.

Some years ago I wrote a curriculum for a BMX based charity focusing on children at risk. The people delivering the program were highly experienced BMX riders. We went through the curriculum before delivery, and they spoke of 'pumping' at the BMX track. I asked what that was, and they proceeded to almost show me whilst sitting at the dining table at a restaurant. I said, "No, explain it to me". That stumped them for a moment, before they started their explanation, throughout which I interjected with questions, such as "At that point, where is your centre of balance?", and "What's the timing of the hip movement?" They had to think deeply about the kinetic chain (see definition immediately below) of the movement they were expecting to be learned by program participants. As to why I am telling you this story, read on.

Kinetic chain – when a joint or segment is in motion, it affects other neighbouring joints and/or segments, forming a human movement pattern. A difference between experienced coaches and novice coaches, is that the experienced or expert coaches observe movement by connected areas, whereas novice coaches tend to observe joint or segment movement in isolation.

Early in this book, I suggested that you were more of a teacher than a coach when dealing with juniors and those new to the sport. This is because you are teaching the fundamental movements to be able to participate in the sport. Many sports require the participant to be able to either catch, throw, run, change direction, swim, cycle, jump, and so on, and probably a few of these hold true to your sport. You need to be able to teach all the required aspects pertinent to your sport to develop the athlete, and not just the "on-field" or "on-court" plays.

This basic-level book cannot go through all the biomechanics of human movement for each sporting activity, so I refer you to sport-specific texts that deal with specific movement.

Is there such a thing as an "ideal" movement? Many sporting textbooks and coaching manuals would have you believe that there is. This is because they need to rely on drawings or pictures, which are not dynamic and usually demonstrate a generalised average of movement to help the reader understand the concept. The reason why a generalised picture or diagram is not ideal is that, for example, an athlete who is 190cms tall with over-average length legs for height will present a very different observation when running compared with an athlete who is 165cms tall with average leg length for height. So your initial observation should leave you with an overall impression or 'feeling' about the quality of the movement, and then focus on specific components.

Task: What individual athlete differences can you identify that will vary your observations?

Here are some: anthropometrics (limb length, height etc), age, gender, experience, training, skill level, flexibility, and fitness level.

Taking our runners as an example, the coach is looking at many visual cues, including head position, are shoulders "warming the ears" or relaxed, arm drive, posture, hip position, deceleration on foot landing, flight time, knee height on recovery, leg turnover rate, coordination, and probably more. Then add the fact that the two runners are of quite different heights and that they will potentially present a different "picture" for evaluation.

So I urge you to research the movements you are teaching to beginners, so that the outcomes reflect the desired movement and do not require re-teaching at a later time, which is not only inefficient but can also leave the athlete frustrated or in the worse case, either injured or drop out of the sport.

Planned Observation

Qualitative evaluation is mostly performed through visual observation. (I'll clarify that shortly, but let's just stick to visual observation for now)

Task: Think for a moment if about whether visual observation is a challenging evaluation process.

What answer did you come up with to the task above? The task of qualitative observation of movement is very challenging, even more so for newer coaches.

Newer coaches struggle with qualitative observation because

103

1. There can be an overwhelming amount of visual information coming in, and the newer coach may not know what incoming information is relevant and what is just "noise"
2. They may also not be physically placing themselves in the best observation position.

Let's talk about these two issues.

To limit the impact of being overwhelmed with incoming visual information, which you are trying to evaluate in real time, so you can make an assessment and provide timely feedback to your athlete, you need to know what the movement should ideally look like and have identified it's critical features and degrees of freedom. In that way, an error of movement will most likely be more obvious during your observation.

> **Task:** Where would you start with the above example using our runners to evaluate technique?

The first step is to plan your observation by identifying the critical features of the movement and then develop an observation plan and recording form (see below).

After developing a sound understanding of the movement or activity, develop a simple table using the critical features you have identified to assist you in focusing your observation of the movement or activity.

For example, if you believe that acceleration (first step quickness) in the first 5-10 metres in field/court sports is a critical skill, our table may look like this:

Critical Skill	Assessment
Foot contact time with the ground	
Stride frequency	
Arm drive	
Body position (centre of gravity)	

Notice, the time the athlete takes to accelerate from a standing start to 5 or 10 metres is not a critical skill, as that is a quantitative measurement. In this section, we are concerned with the process to achieving the outcome, not the outcome in it's own right.

If you can locate videos that show errors with associated explanations, all the better. Ideally, those explanations would also discuss the flow-on effects of the error, as well as the origin of the observed error. Some videos may also have the video loaded into bio-mechanical software for analysis, which adds so much more information to your understanding.

A much overlooked resource to aid your knowledge acquisition are other coaches in different sports. For example, if you coach a sport that involves explosive running, why not go to an athletics track, approach a sprints coach and ask if they mind you observing what they do, and if they can spare a few minutes afterward for a chat. The worst that will happen is that they say "No", the best is that they recognise a coach from another sport who has recognised gaps in their knowledge and would like to go some way to plugging those gaps. When I was involved with lacrosse, I attended national track coaching seminars to further my understanding, as lacrosse involved bursts of explosive acceleration. You would also pick up some excellent athlete warm-up information for sprints.

Observe

The importance of your observation position should not be underestimated. A different observation position relative to your athlete's position may provide different information to you. Take a moment to think about the coach that stands on the sideline or on the pool deck end, never shifting, always observing from the same vantage point. Are they maximising the amount of qualitative information they are collecting?

There are three critical elements to help you focus your attention when observing an athlete's movement:
1. Know exactly what to look for (knowledge of which discrete elements to observe)
2. Know when to look (observation timed with the movement)
3. Know how long to observe for (long enough to allow time to gather information, but not too long to start gathering extraneous information)

As an exercise, observe an athlete running or swimming past you at right angles, then observe the same athlete running/swimming towards you, and then again running/swimming away from you. What types of information would you plan to collect in each of the three observation positions?

Similarly, your proximity to the athlete being assessed is also important. If you're close, it may be difficult to see the whole athlete; too far away, and it may be difficult to see a particular component of the movement. As a rule of thumb, the faster the movement, the greater the viewing distance from the athlete. Normal speed movement observation distance is usually 5-10 metres, sprint movement would normally be about 20 metres distant. For some movement assessment with immediate intervention, you will need to be close enough to the athlete to be able to provide touch, visual or verbal cues as required. So what would you do for the movement you are assessing?

It is also important to minimise distractions when observing your athlete. Distractions will interfere with your ability to gather and process relevant information.

If it's appropriate to the evaluation, use fixed vertical and/or horizontal references.

For less complex skills, I'd start my observations from a distance where I could see the whole movement. Having made myself fully conversant with the movements critical features, including the sequencing beforehand, I'd focus on any error "pops". This concentration in my field of view of the component I wish to focus my observation on, filters out extraneous information coming into my observation field, thereby reducing my visual and auditory information loading.

If the skill I'm observing is complex in nature, I'd limit my observation to separate components within the overall skill. I'd base that observational skill distillation on both identified critical features and on the precedence of movement.

Taking the observation of individual components forward, the coach needs to look for unnecessary movement within the action, for example, a "bobbing head" when running, or during backstroke swimming. The directions of the moving parts need to be observed, as moving parts change the athlete's balance, direction of applied force, centre of gravity, centre of mass, and can also demonstrate oppositional movement.

As you observe the athlete's range of motion (ROM), you are looking for both an appropriate ROM (too much is as problematic as too little) as well as a continuous flow of motion, not jerky or stop/start.

You also mustn't forget that qualitative observation also includes using all your senses including: visually observing the athlete as well as listening to the athlete's touch points, eg, how loud their foot strike is when running, etc.

To summarise, you need to observe the athlete's movement and compare it to the desired movement as well as using your other senses to complete the observation.

Evaluation

Your initial response when evaluating a movement should be based upon an overall impression or feeling about the quality of the movement, after which you then look at the specific critical skill components. Remember also that you are diagnosing a movement judged against a range of correctness, whilst allowing for individual variation between athletes.

Let's assume that you have a reasonable understanding of what the movement you are going to observe should look like, be it a vault in gymnastics, recovery arm movement in freestyle, a bat swing in baseball, etc. You observe your athlete executing the movement and observe an error. (We'll keep this error as generic, so you can insert the error you observe)

This observation happens in real time and could be performed very quickly. Depending on how you process visual information, you could take a video so you can replay the movement at varying speeds, or maybe you can "replay" the mental video captured in your "mind's eye". Using a sequential method, the aim is to compare your "image' of the desirable phases of the movement with the information you gather through your observation. You can also use a mechanical method, depending on what you are observing, which involves evaluating the observed motor skills that directly relate to corrections that can improve performance, such as sequential coordination, range of movement, etc.

However, what you observe may not be the actual error. How can it be that you identify an error, but that isn't the error? This sounds counterintuitive.

There are two possible reasons an identified error is not the actual error.
1. To understand a movement, you need to understand the kinetic chain of the action. In other words:
    a) You need to understand and be able to identify the movement of both its components and the movement in its entirety.
    b) How the various elements of the movement are interconnected and influence each other.

c) Recognise the precedence of movement, or otherwise you may be observing an artefact of an earlier movement segment/sequence.
2. The athlete is still developing the coordination to execute the movement.

The principal question relating to the first point above is – how well do you understand the movement? This includes elements such as: balance; what is the origin of the movement (feet, hips, shoulder etc); what are the precedence's within the chain of movement (which comes first, or are there two or more elements that coordinate simultaneously to form the movement; speed of the movement and is that speed variable, or is the speed linear, or does it build throughout the movement? You need to know at least these basic elements to be able to assess the quality of the movement. To take the notion of an artefact further, it is vital to know if the outcome of your observation has any relationship to any previous action to ensure your corrective feedback is accurate.

As a new or newer coach, error identification that may be related to a previous action can be problematic to identify due to:
- A difficulty in relating a bio-mechanical action to a previous bio-mechanical action, and how the segments interact
- In determining if the bio-mechanical error is related to a non-bio-mechanical action, such as the athlete's vision or vision focus, or their mental/physical preparedness.

The origin of the movement is arguably the most critical to know. This allows you to assess the quality of the movement by breaking the whole assessment down into bite-sized sections and this then allows you to form the complete movement chain. That may sound simple, but let's take a moment.

A simplistic breakdown of throwing a ball – does it start with the feet or moving the throwing arm backwards to a "cocked" position, or a multi-factor action including hip rotation and visual attention? Perhaps these occur simultaneously? But if I'm moving my feet into a throwing position and my throwing arm backwards, what are my hips doing? And my shoulders? And my torso alignment? What will the weight transfer look like from the ground up as I throw in relation to my whole body movement? What would a coordinated throw look like?

Similarly, let's look at running in a field sport. How does arm drive relate to leg drive? Is hip stability a good reference point for efficiency evaluation, head stability, is dorsi-flexion of the ankle to obtain an elastic pre-load important; knee height, hip drive, shoulder position, overall posture? (That's a shortened list.)

In summary, movement errors can be caused by four key areas that a coach must evaluate:
1. Critical ability – strength, endurance, flexibility
2. Skill performance deficit – technique, perception, decision-making errors
3. Biomechanical and movement sequencing errors
4. Motivation and attitude

As you read above, there are many individual aspects to create a coordinated quality movement, all of which you need to be able to see and evaluate to determine the movement, and above all, which element is affecting that movement, causing it to be less than ideal. So, break down the movement into its component parts and understand the movement pattern and precedence – a bit like developing a Gantt chart.

Once you have understood and implemented the above movement breakdown with associated precedence, you can then utilise that information to commence your athlete movement evaluation, and then implement an appropriate intervention strategy if required.

Intervention

The intervention strategy may include: specific strength development (eg core strength); implementation of drills which segment the desired action allowing only a component of the movement to be the focus and then integrating that back into the whole movement; video review with the athlete so they can see what you have identified; physically moving the athlete's limb/hand etc through the desired movement (kinaesthetic); verbally telling them what you need in the movement; having them watch another athlete perform the movement correctly. The methodology of your intervention will also relate to your understanding of the athletes preferred learning style.

As you are most likely working with younger athletes, it is also likely that they are still learning the required movements from an early stage. It is also worth noting that in my experience, some athletes who hit a growth spurt tend to lose some coordination for a short time. As they are learning a new movement, they are forming new neural connections and pathways, which take time to develop and to be able to coordinate the movement. Over time, these neural connections and pathways will also have the effect of the athlete activating more of the desired muscle groups and less of the antagonist group, creating a more coordinated movement associated with more applied power availability.

A lack of coordination can also be inadvertently developed by the coach through not instigating an adequate preparation program for the movement, through the use of drills. It can also be that the athlete has not developed the strength to be able to control the movement, which may also be a coaching programming issue.

Intervention strategy

Once you have identified, evaluated, and diagnosed any issue with an athlete's movement, an intervention strategy would be put in place.

In the evaluation of any change your intervention has brought about, you must remember to position yourself where you can observe and provide feedback effectively. The feedback can be either instructions to alter movement and/or reinforcing good aspects of the movement performance with positive reinforcement.

There are two types of feedback the athlete will be receiving – extrinsic and intrinsic. For example, as the coach, you will be providing verbal feedback (extrinsic), which is as a type of augmented feedback. The other feedback the athlete receives is what they 'feel', which is referred to as intrinsic feedback.

As a coach, you provide augmented feedback, which is the primary mode of intervention. Key components to consider in your augmented feedback include:
- Don't provide an information overload by providing too much feedback at a time

- Ensure your feedback is specific to allow the athlete to focus on an element
- The feedback should be provided within an immediate time frame
- The feedback should be positive, which should include the use of positive language, as well as positive body language and delivered with enthusiasm
- Your language should be consistent and use 'cue' words and phrases
- If your intervention is not yielding change, alter your approach

This process should be delivered in an encouraging environment at all times, and the athlete shouldn't feel that they are being singled out. This can be assured by engaging with the athlete using age appropriate language so that they understand the reasoning behind your intervention. This engagement starts the pathway to coach independence for your athlete by educating them in the correct movement through shared knowledge, which is empowering to the athlete and helps deepen the coach/athlete relationship by power sharing.

Remember at all times, the athlete's development is a direct product of your intervention, so an unsuccessful intervention means you, as the coach, need to reassess your intervention method for that athlete. It is not a sign of coach weakness to admit to your athlete that your intervention hasn't yielded the result you were after and that you are changing your strategy – it is a sign of coach maturity and confidence, and better engages with your athlete by informing them that you will instigate a different strategy to continue their development.

Analysing qualitative data

There are several ways to analyse qualitative data. Firstly, you could just leave it as a visual input from which you make decisions; or you could video the movement and enter it into bio-mechanical software for analysis; or thirdly, you could quantify the data into numbers. As this is an early stage in a career coaching book, I'll describe the above in broad brush strokes, as a "taster" for you to explore further if you wish.

First, however, don't get too carried away with data analysis of either quantitative or qualitative data, as you may end up in a position of "Paralysis by analysis", with lots of data collected, turned into volumes of information with no idea of what to do next due to overload.

There's no need to discuss the process of simple visual inspection of movement against a known correct range of movement, as that's been discussed earlier in this chapter, except for the question of "What is the correct movement"?

I've already written that texts and coursework books tend to depict only one correct movement pattern for any given movement. This, of course, is limited by the non-dynamic nature of a text, and the depiction expresses the ideal as it is at the time of publication.

The critical takeaway from this is that athletic movement changes over time. These changes may be brought about by rule changes in the sport or by bio-mechanical advances, finding efficiencies through research, but still staying within the sports rules.

Task: What defines a correct movement?

My view is that a correct movement fulfils the following criteria:
1. The movement is within the rules of the sport
2. The movement is bio-mechanically efficient
3. The movement does not create injury or a platform for future injury
4. The movement fulfils the requirement it is meant to, eg, throw a ball accurately, run, etc

The above does leave it a little open as to a definitively correct movement, so what we end up with is a range of acceptable movement that meets the above criteria. That provides the coach with a broader range of acceptable motion that is visually captured; however, this makes it somewhat more difficult to analyse the correctness of movement.

So for our qualitative analysis we end up with a singular definitive reference movement (the text book reference) and then apply a + or − to that movement in minuscule degrees of change until we reach a threshold where the movement becomes problematic to the other key considerations indicated above: rules, efficiency, fit for purpose, and/or injury potential. You then arrive at a small window of acceptable movement, which you apply in your analysis.

You should also bear in mind that some of your athletes may lack flexibility, strength or coordination at this time and that they are a "work in progress" when applying your evaluation model.

If you are able access bio-mechanical software to assist with your analysis, you first need to ask yourself, "Is it necessary, or am I just adding to my workload without really value adding to my decision making"? However, it can be quite fun to have a "play" within this type of software, as it can add a great deal to your understanding of the movement you are evaluating. For example, a horizontal line drawn across the screen to determine the knee height (or differential knee height) during the recovery phase of a running action could be of use; a line drawn "through" the spine compared with a vertical line can show degrees of lean; a time-base can give you flight time in running, and so on. Interesting, but does it add value to your program for this level athlete?

A way to quantify the movement you observe is to draw a grid with columns marked across the top with the key individual elements you are observing. These observations are graded with a score, for example, 0 for correct, -1 for within range but needs work, -2 for borderline on edge of the range, -3 out of range, -4 for way out of range. This allows you to track the athlete's development in their development towards a correct range of movement. Initially, you may find this to be a little haphazard, with your observation scores not always being consistent. That's OK, as you're learning too. Over time, your scored evaluation will become consistent and a valuable assessment tool.

I urge you to give the above a go, even if you don't initially find it of great value or you have difficulty in quick observation and evaluation, you will improve over time. Your development of speed of observation and evaluation will really benefit your coaching, as you will be able to provide timely, almost instantaneous feedback to your athlete. It will also help you to focus on the movement components that are critical to establishing the overall movement and improve your understanding of the kinetic chain of the movement with the associated precedences.

Quantitative evaluation

There are six fundamental questions to answer about measuring quantitative performance:

1. Why do you want to measure?
2. What are you going to measure?
3. Is it necessary to measure (this is not the same as "why")?
4. How are you going to measure?
5. How are you going to interpret the results?
6. What are you going to do with the results?

Task: Answer all six questions above before proceeding.

There are two types of testing available to the coach. In its simplest form, quantitative (objective) testing can be defined as a method where data is collected using instruments (an exact quantifiable amount) such as stopwatches, tape measures, force platforms, etc, which provide an exact measurement. The other form of testing is qualitative (subjective) measurement, which, as the name suggests, is subjective by design and measures the "quality" of movement as discussed earlier. There is also a cross-over where movement can be captured digitally as a video, entered into biomechanical software, and analysed using both quantitative and qualitative methods.

Quantitative Testing.

The application of quantitative testing requires you to answer several questions first.

- Do you need to test?
- Is it age-appropriate? Is it too complex for the athlete to understand, or too physically or emotionally demanding?

- Fully understand the "why" you are using a particular test
- Fully understand the "what" you are testing for
- The selected test must make sense. Does the test directly relate to the physiologic or other demands of the sport?
- Can you apply the test? Do you know the test protocol, do you have the right and reliable measuring equipment, and an appropriate testing space?
- Can you interpret the data correctly to be able to gain useful information that you can apply?
- How will you use the information to enhance your coaching output?

Quantitative testing refers to testing where the data collected is definitive and not necessarily open to an alternate viewpoint, although it may be statistically interpreted differently.

Notice I refer to the collected numbers as "data", not as "information". Information is garnered through the interpretation of the collected data via statistical means. You shouldn't be put off by the notion of using statistics in your coaching. But a word of caution, you must use the correct statistical method to retrieve useful information that you can legitimately apply. An incorrect statistical application will also yield an answer! You also need to understand the "what" and "why" of your testing to be able to apply meaningful intervention into your coaching program.

Remember also that the data you collect is a snapshot in time on that particular day. The same test run within a few days may yield a slightly different result, which could be due to the athlete's state of energy, hydration, alertness, motivation, environment, etc. So, if the same test can yield a different result a few days later, how is that of use?

Testing is useful as it provides comparative information taken over a medium to long term to show trends. So become familiar with the following simple statistics to get you started (and remember, these are usually available in any spreadsheet application as pre-loaded formulae):

- Mean
- Median
- Slope of curve (y=Mx+c)
- Rate of decay (for maximal repeated efforts within a test set)

With the correct type of data and with a little more understanding, you can add regression analysis to the list, but that is usually of use at the higher end of athletic development measurement and probably not where you will be at the moment.

At what age should you start quantitative performance testing?

As a new or newer coach, you will most likely be coaching a younger or inexperienced group of athletes. So is quantitative testing necessary?

The questions you must ask include:

- Is running formal testing the best way to quantify performance improvement?
- Do I need to quantify performance improvement?
- Is it beneficial to the athlete's development to be involved in a test protocol?

There is a caveat to this section, in that it may also be sport-dependant. In a sport such as competitive swimming, young swimmers perform against a pace clock or are involved in regular "time trials" as a normal part of the training environment. This can occur from ages as young as 8, or even less. In many instances, they also compete year-round, so "test data" from competition is in plentiful supply. This competition data would also be available in athletics. This is often not available in other sports, where the only data would be on the scoreboard (assuming scores are kept).

Let me take a moment and put my "coaching hat on". Would I run a test protocol with 9-year-olds? My simple answer is "No", it simply is not age-appropriate (not withstanding my swimming example above). We could discuss this by adding a year at a time, but trying to arrive at a definitive age-based start point is nonsensical. In very general terms, my view is about 14 years of age for boys and 13 years of age for girls would probably be appropriate, perhaps even a year earlier. The potential loading from maximal testing is high, and in my opinion, post-pubescent athletes would be at an appropriate developmental level to participate. The caveat to this goes back to the first point in the opening list – why do you want to test in the first place?

Three very important points the coach should consider in their decision regarding quantitative testing in their program are:
1. Whatever test you decide to implement, it must be relevant and repeatable.
2. The tests must be incorporated into your seasonal plan, not an ad-hoc addition to your program design.
3. Tests are not a form of punishment. I cannot emphasise this enough. I've heard coaches run a "beep test" as a form of

punishment. This is an unacceptable coaching practice and demonstrates that the coach may have lost their way.

You must also pay regard to the type of test you are contemplating having in your program, as in my first point above. For example, testing for aerobic endurance would not make much sense if no aerobic endurance training has taken place (other than perhaps to obtain an initial base measure). The results would simply show that your programming has not developed this physiology.

Thoughts on when testing could take place within a training program will be covered in the "training planning" section of this book.

Control your test environment.

A fundamental of quantitative testing (and being able to compare repeated test results over time) is to ensure consistency, as best as possible of, the test conditions. For example, any changes in ambient temperature, humidity, wind, time of day, or testing surface will colour your results from a comparative perspective. That won't render the test data invalid, but you must consider the impact any test condition changes may have, and make notes accordingly. Environmental elements are outside your control, and it may be, that you test in different seasons, so variances in environmental elements should be an accepted part of your results interpretation.

The above identified some of the more obvious external considerations that may colour your results. However, there are less obvious elements that can colour test results, such as:

- Alteration to pretesting warm-up. The use of the same warm-up for the same testing session is important, as it provides you with the athletes in the same state of readiness to perform as they were for the previous testing sessions. Note: Different tests may require different warm-up protocols. A short discussion is further below.
- Knowing your athlete's physical and mental preparedness is a must. For example, running a test set on a Monday may seem to make sense, as it's the start of the week, but for older athletes, some may have had late nights over the weekend which may impact their performance resulting in incorrect results interpretation. It is also worth considering that some post-pubescent female athletes may have a physical and/or emotional impact on their potential performance depending on where in their cycle they are.

Warm-up protocol for testing

I mentioned that the same warm-up protocol should be used for the same test set, as it forms part of the test conditions. This is one element entirely in your control. But why?

> **Task**: Think about what the warm-up protocol would look like in two types of test scenarios: one being for a sprint test, the other an endurance test. How would they differ?

Using the same warm-up for the same test protocol ensures the athletes are in as close physical and emotional state of readiness as can be compared with previous times. This means that they are physically in the same state as is their anxiety level. (Anxiety in this context is defined as an emotional state of readiness, not a level of fear) If the warm-up protocol is considerably different, there is a possibility that the athletes will be in a different state of readiness to perform, thereby colouring your data. It is also likely that over repeated test exposures, the athlete's nervousness will diminish as they become more familiar with the process, which will have a positive impact on their potential performance.

The first element in my athlete warm-up protocol for a test session is to explain to the athletes what we are testing for, the test format, and how I will use that information to better develop my programming through this snap-shot. It is not a measure of their performance as such, but a part of developing the coaching/athlete process to continue along the improvement line. This is the first step in the athlete's engagement in the process. Sharing this information also empowers the athlete to become more engaged in their development through increased understanding, which will lead to better, informed discussions between you as the coach and the athlete.

The warm-up protocol for a test session is conceptually no different from any other warm-up in that we are getting our athletes ready to perform. So how does the coach do that?

Firstly, you must understand what you are testing. By that, I mean, are you testing for endurance, repeated sprints, acceleration, and agility? It is also worth noting that it is unwise to test for aerobic and anaerobic (eg, max repeat sprints) on the same day due to the physiologic stress and recovery requirements to run successful and meaningful tests.

The warm-up should reflect the energy and neural systems the athletes will be engaging in the intensity required during the test. The warm-up should also ensure that the athletes have fully recovered energy/neural systems to be able to perform the tests to the best of their ability, in other words, be fatigue-free before testing.

To ensure a fatigue-free athlete, you should pay attention to the intensity and duration of the warm-up. It is also imperative that once the athlete is warmed up, that they are not allowed to cool down, with the associated cooling of musculature, joints, and the "slowing back down" of the neural system. This is of particular importance for tests involving high stress, such as maximal efforts.

For example, when I performed a high stress maximal effort test for sub-elite water polo, the warm-up consisted of a dry land warm-up, general swim warm-up of 400 metres, then a series of progressively faster short sprints of 12-15 metres with swim through with a full rest between, followed by a ten minute quiet sit down recovery while being kept warm, before a maximal 12x25 metre, 5 second rest each end, push start, maximal swim test. Therefore, the warm-up reflected the systems which will be stressed during the test to ensure those systems were energised and available from the start. The short sprints during the warm-up "fired up" the neural system to a high level of activation. (OK, the last two sentences are a bit simplistic, but this is a beginner coaching book, so it's important to understand the overall concept more than the chemistry behind it)

A warm-up moving from general to high intensity with appropriate recovery pretest would also be used for agility testing due to the high stress demands placed upon the muscular and joint structures to both supply and deliver high levels of burst power (both for the athlete to generate maximal power for performance and to minimise the risk of injury from putting high stresses through ill-prepared muscles and joints).

If you're running aerobic testing, say a 5,000+ metre run or a 2,000 metre swim, then a lighter aerobic warm-up would be suitable. Due to the nature of the time taken for an aerobic test (although this is applicable to all testing), the athletes need to be fully hydrated and fuelled before commencement. As a coach, you need to ensure your athletes are properly prepared and that you do not defer that responsibility to the athlete before they can fully take on that responsibility.

Process vs results.

As much as over the years the notion of keeping score, acknowledging individual performances, etc, with juniors has declined, not surprisingly though, the athletes usually have an idea. After all, it's called competitive sport for a reason. Depending on where you coach in the world, keeping score etc, is slowly introduced as the athlete matures. As you are most likely coaching older juniors and assuming your quantitative testing has passed the "appropriate for your particular cohort test", what do you do with the data?

If you've explained to the athletes the purpose of the testing is to provide you with information that you can use to produce programming appropriate to their current needs by identifying gaps, then they shouldn't be concerned with their results. It may be difficult for them not to know their results, as they may be interested to know, or perhaps a well-meaning parent on the sideline happens to time the run, for example, and passes the information onto their child. The athlete mustn't focus on the result as an end in itself, nor should you, as the coach, in conversation with the athlete.

So there are two clear process-based aspects:
1. The process of testing provides a feedback mechanism for your program development.
2. Using the information to have the athlete understand that the test results are a building block in the management of their overall development, and not a defining statistic.

Results and your athlete

You've decided to collect quantitative and qualitative data for your program management, but how do you include the athlete in the discussion, or don't you?

> **Task:** If you decide to include your athlete in the discussion, how would you go about it? How would you manage an athlete's perceived "under-performance"? Or conversely, what would the discussion sound like if the athlete performed beyond expectation? And, whose expectations is the athlete performing to?

You have no program without an athlete (or a group of athletes), so you are dependent upon them for your program, and they are dependent upon you for their athletic development. If you accept a mutual dependence, then it follows that they are an intrinsic component of this discussion.

The environment you establish for this discussion is an important component of your relationship with your athlete. It should be pointed out that a formal discussion is not always necessary. For example, if you program a 'star agility test', everyone will know their timed results during the performance, so feedback is on the spot and would normally revolve around body positioning, foot speed, and balance to improve performance between trials. What I am referring to here is a broader discussion with the athlete about overall performance and development, which would be more applicable to the older athlete.

It may be that you wish to address the athletes as a group and talk in general terms about the results. There are several things to bear in mind when addressing a group:

- Don't have them looking into the sun; you don't want them to feel under the "spotlight of interrogation".
- If they are seated, you should also be seated if possible; similarly, if they are standing, then you should be standing. This ensures a more egalitarian communication environment.
- Address all the athletes, moving your gaze. Do not rest your gaze on any one athlete during any one sentence; otherwise, that athlete will think you are addressing them.
- Keep it short and succinct.
- If it's the first time the test is run, the talk should revolve around the positives of participation and how the baseline measures will be used.
- If it's a repeated test, keep enthusiastic, even if the results were less than what you expected. Remember, the results are most likely a factor of your programming.
- Don't be over-enthusiastic either. If the results were below your expectations, don't pretend and build the emotion up; the athletes will realise it's fake. Similarly, if the results are above expectations, don't get too upbeat, as it may create a false sense of future expectations, as well as create a coaching environment built on extrinsic motivation. Also,

if you get too over-enthusiastic, where can you go from there if next time it's even better?
- Lastly, let them know that the information will guide you to further their athletic development.

Addressing an individual athlete is more complex, as it becomes a debrief discussion. I contend that an individual debrief may not be appropriate for juniors (in age), but could start with 12/13-yr-olds. This age group usually starts showing an inclination towards one sport, as they've moving from sport sampling towards being involved in only one or two sports, or it may be they are only involved in one sport from an earlier age, engaged all year round and becoming early stage specialised, then perhaps the results debrief age could be lower.

A discussion with an athlete is most likely to be informal and only last a few minutes at most. It may also be that a parent/caregiver is also present, which is not an issue, just remember you are talking to the athlete, not the parent/caregiver. Keep the conversation on topic. Three possibilities drive the discussion: under-performance, expected performance, and performance above expectation.

Remember, I am not just referring to quantitative measures, but also qualitative measures of movement in the discussion.

Key points when discussing under-performance:
- How the performance relates to the expected performance
- Do not apportion or direct blame
- Listen carefully to what the athlete says
- Be genuine and encouraging at all times; they are still developing in the sport

- Relate the performance to the development process, not to the discrete performance as such (eg, still developing strength/power in that element of the movement; still developing first step quickness; still developing aerobic capacity, etc)
- Present an individualised, realistic development plan to the athlete to address outcomes as part of the development process
- Explain the concept of non-linear performance development, requiring different systems and attributes to be developed and work together ,which usually does not occur concurrently

Key points when discussing expected performance:
- Ask the athlete how they perceive the results
- Discuss that the athlete is tracking as expected and relate that to the athlete development plan
- Discuss future expectations and how you, as the coach, intend to assist the athlete in meeting those expectations
- Be positive and encouraging, as they may believe that they may have been able to perform better

Key points when discussing performance above expectation:
- Ask the athlete how they perceive the results
- Athlete's systems (neural, energy, power, etc) responding well to training stimulus
- Explain that the step up in performance is not a sustainable linear line with an upward trajectory to 'infinity', but now needs to be consolidated
- The athlete development plan will be slightly revised based on new information

- Explain what their development plan will look like going forward

As indicated in the above discussions, they should generally be limited to the older cohort. Working with sub-juniors/juniors, the focus is on qualitative analysis to further their movement development, which may not be directly shared with them beyond encouragement as a part of the development process. Verbal interactions with juniors should always be within a positive context, never focusing on outcomes but rather focusing on processes and the enjoyment of participation.

Quantitative data collected, now what?

You've run your quantitative test/s and collected data written on paper, or maybe entered directly into a spreadsheet. All went well.

On the assumption that you utilised test protocols appropriate to the physiology you want to test for, then the data gives you direct information about the efficacy of the training stimulus you are providing to your athletes.

For example, if the coach has run a six week aerobic endurance program and has found no change in aerobic endurance in the athletes from the previous to current tests, it can be assumed that the programming provided has not been effective in increasing aerobic endurance. Or does it? There can be alternate explanations:
- An invalid test for aerobic endurance was used
- The data collection was incorrect (eg, incorrectly measured total distance used to conduct the two tests)

- Environmental differences (if outside: wind speed, temperature, etc)
- The programming provided didn't stress the aerobic system enough to elicit a response
- The programming intensity stressed the anaerobic system instead, which wasn't sensitive to the test being applied.

Similarly, if you run an agility test, but haven't spent any time on, say, first step quickness, fast foot ladders, teaching the athletes how to pivot, and so on, is it realistic to expect an improvement?

The first step is to review the data alongside your programming. This is only possible if you write down every training session in advance, and then add notes after each session if needed. I always wrote all my programs into yearly diaries, which had the advantage of having a yearly single-page calendar at the front, allowing me to design the annual outline of the physiological focus week by week.

If you do this too, the review will be easy and you will very quickly start to understand what programming has been effective. It will also allow you to manage the ramp-up of workload at an appropriate rate to provide the correct stimulus level. Appropriate ramp-up of workload is critical, too much too fast will likely cause injury, diminishing interest by the athletes, illness and/or over-training syndrome. Not enough increase in stimulus will not yield any or, at best, a diminished improvement to what could have been achieved, or even de-training.

As you review your programming, let's assume it's yielded athletic improvement in what you are measuring and you have decided that you wish to continue to improve that parameter. You may be inclined to just continue on an upward trajectory of workload from where you left off, after all why would you want to go slightly backwards in stimulus? The reason is that the concept of overload requires recovery to allow for supercompensation and improvement. Athletic development is not linear but step-wise, with slight rises followed by short plateaus to allow for adaptation to occur.

You need to develop the whole athlete in this context, that is, all energy systems. There is a caveat here, though. Preadolescent athletes are aerobic dominant with an immature anaerobic system, so trying to stress the anaerobic system with this cohort will only cause the athlete stress with no real results.

This fundamental is critical. You must also remember, your junior athletes are not "small adults" and they will most likely be at differing stages of maturational development even if they are the same chronological age.

The collected data could be entered into a spreadsheet for easy retrieval and data manipulation. I saved my spreadsheet to the cloud, which allowed me to retrieve the data from any device, anywhere I was. It also afforded data protection in case, for example, my laptop's drive stopped working, thereby rendering my data irretrievable.

How complex you want to go is up to you. With my younger athletes, I simply entered the test or competition data along a line from their name, under an appropriate column header. For the older athletes, they each had their own tab within a spreadsheet. My sub-elite athletes had their own spreadsheet within a team folder, which allowed me to perform more advanced data evaluation and graphing, which I would then either email as a PDF to the athlete with accompanying notes, or print and go through the analysis with them in person.

So you've collected the quantitative data that you wanted, assuming you have decided that it is a useful thing to do with the athlete cohort you are in charge of developing. The next item on your agenda is how to incorporate the information from the data into your coaching.

The qualitative and quantitative information you have collected, either formally or informally, provides you with the feedback on how you are tracking in the development of your athletes in the various key areas of conditioning (ie, aerobic, anaerobic, strength, power etc) and movement development (ie coordinated limb and body movement, balance, etc).

As a coach, you need to be aware of the efficacy of your programming. Your program efficacy is more than just the scoreboard result, which, for example, in a field sport, only means you outperformed your opponents in terms of goals/runs scored. This is a short-term outcome-focused view, when you should be more process-focused in the long-term development of your athlete.

Beyond the artificial testing environment, the game day or competitive meet is the real-world acid test, which demonstrates the preparation of your athletes. Coaches in sports such as swimming, athletics, softball, etc, where they can focus on an individual performance, can more easily assess the athlete's performance on numerous parameters to feed back into their development program. In sports with a concentration of activity involving a whole team (eg, football, netball, hockey, etc), individual performances can be more difficult to assess, as an individuals skill performance can be dependent on a team dynamic or how the game provides opportunities. There are also additional stressors placed upon the individual's application of game sense and decision making. However, the "fitness" development you have programmed will be assessable.

One of the challenges facing team based sport coaches is having enough time available within the allocated training sessions to be able to program skill development/coordination and game sense development with enough time available to develop the fitness attributes required of the sport including aerobic, anaerobic, strength, prehabilitation, agility and then added to that managing developing athletes at potentially different maturational and developmental stages.

You also need to be aware of the time taken for "fitness" changes to manifest through changes in blood chemistry, neural network and intracellular changes (these will not be covered in detail as they are beyond this books' scope) so that your periodised training program aligns, with enough time allowed as well, so as not to ramp up the workload too fast. Your programming must also be fit for purpose based on the age group – young athletes are not "mini-adults".

With the collected information you can then adjust your programming accordingly to ensure the right amount of stress is applied to your athletes to continue their development in all aspects of the sport's requirements.

Physical Preparation of your Athlete

The focus of this chapter will be on the development of the energy systems, which is often referred to in general terms simply as "fitness development".

To continue the stated philosophy underpinning this book, the explanations for developing the various energy systems will be kept as basic as possible while still maintaining meaning, and that you will be able to apply those concepts in your coaching. I will include some cellular and chemistry information; however, it will be explained in a way that is easily understood and that you will have confidence to apply the reasoning to your training protocols. It is intended that you will also have the basic understanding to be able to explain your program structure to your athletes, so they too can understand your rationale and better engage. To those coaches who have an understanding of blood chemistry, etc, I apologise for what will appear to be theory gaps; however, the aim is not to "blind" readers with science, but to provide concise and basic information that is easily understood and can be applied.

As a coach, your primary objectives are to develop and deliver training programs that will improve your athlete/s performance and cause no harm in that process. The three components to achieve this are: the individual athlete, the training program, and the delivery time frames (periodisation).

The outcomes of your training program to help the athlete achieve their potential depend on both the physical and psychological readiness of the individual athlete. The physical readiness refers to the physical maturation of the athlete, which is not the same for all athletes if based only upon their chronological age.

Within a group of junior athletes, they will likely reach puberty at different chronological ages with the associated alterations to hormones, which implies that one athlete's readiness for certain types of work (eg, strength work, lactate tolerance work) may be more advanced than another athlete's readiness within your cohort.

To add to the difficulty of programming for a group of athletes, you will find some of your athletes will have different responses to the stimulus you provide, even if they all apply themselves equally. This is due to some athletes being classified as "responders", that is, their physiology is more sensitive to the stimulus you provide and will show a higher level of adaptation. However, all athletes will show a response/adaptation to varying degrees. These variances in response can include:
- Existing level of conditioning
- Genetics
- Age
- Gender
- Responder vs non-responder

Similarly, the psychological readiness is also likely to vary within your athlete cohort. This variance can exhibit itself as the athlete's level of commitment and their psychological resilience to accept higher workloads.

Another important point for consideration, which can be challenging, is how to manage the differences in the individual responses of athletes when exposed to the same training program stimulus while ensuring all athletes remain engaged and continue to develop towards their potential, with no athlete being under- or over-trained.

You have three broad elements for athlete preparation to develop within your role as a coach:
1. Performance skills – teach/refine/develop the skills the athlete requires to be able to participate in the sport, eg, running, agility, catching, swimming etc
2. Psychological skills – decision making, confidence development, resilience, and be able to train to compete
3. Physical preparation to train and compete (this chapter's focus) – developing the energy and neural systems, range of motion of movement within the sports' requirements, strength and power, etc, all to support the performance skills.

Core stability

This will be a very short section, as there are many views on this matter, many with differing views or interpretations. It is also quite complex by nature and requires an expert understanding to program and implement. I'm not suggesting that basic 'core' stability work should not be undertaken, but to caution that for a new/newer coach 'core' deficiencies can be difficult to identify correctly and rectify without both a high level of knowledge and the commitment and understanding of the athlete.

Core stability usually refers to being able to keep the pelvis and lower back in positions that are able to produce and transmit forces, while maintaining an acceptable alignment to minimise injury risk.

There is a second 'core girdle' – the pectoral girdle. The focus is on scapula (shoulder blade) stability (this may also be referred to as shoulder or rotator cuff stability). As many sports have a throwing/hitting/arm movement element, the pectoral girdle is also important

The key-word is stability. Core stability is very difficult to measure and is specific to a movement pattern. You may research the internet to find core stability tests that you may want to apply, to then identify deficiencies and put a remedial program in place. Some athletes fail all stability tests and never get injured. Some athletes work hard at core stability and end up with a rock-hard torso/core and can perform tricks while standing on a Swiss ball, but have no stabilisation in their sporting technique. Introducing a Swiss ball or Pilates does not automatically teach someone trunk muscle coordination in a dynamic situation.

The coach's knowledge of the 'stretch-shorten cycle' and the 'kinetic chain' is critical to understanding forces applied through a movement. For example, if the muscles in the trunk aren't strong enough or are not engaged at the right time, the generated force will get redirected, diminishing performance as well as creating stress to parts of the body not designed for that stress loading.

The question arises: Should you, as a coach, have your athletes perform 'trunk core' or 'pectoral core' strengthening exercises? The short answer is probably. However you must understand several things: they are not a solution for poor technique; it will not create a superior athlete for you; they need to be performed with the athlete's awareness of the muscular focus of the work; you need to ensure you are not creating other issues by creating an imbalance; you need to know the purpose.

As far as pectoral core work is concerned, rotator cuff work with bands has been a part of swimming for decades as an attempt to avoid shoulder injuries. It is also used in throwing sports (baseball, softball, javelin, etc).

To summarise, core work is used in an attempt to minimise injuries, maximise force in the desired direction with minimal loss, and to create stability. I would conclude by saying there is no definitive evidence of absolute efficacy guaranteed, it is not a substitute for ensuring your athlete has correct technique with correct neuromuscular engagement, with as minimal as possible antagonist engagement. (antagonist – muscles not involved in the movement, or muscles engaged that are contrary to the movement)

Warm-up and cool down

The role of warm-up is to:

a) Increase body temperature which increases the elasticity of tendons, muscles, and ligaments, and allows for a greater muscular force to be applied with less injury risk.
b) Increase respiration and heart rate.
c) To engage and activate neural pathways for the upcoming work in both intensity and speed of movement.
d) To reflect the intensity of the upcoming work sets or competition.
e) Should be dynamic, including dynamic stretching once "warmed up".
f) Should have enough time allowed to be effective.

g) Should build in intensity to an appropriate level reflecting the upcoming work.

h) Should be progressive by design (increasing in intensity during the warm-up activities).

i) Should include drills, for example, "A" skips, "B" skips, etc, run-throughs, fast foot ladders, mini-hurdles, etc, for sports involving running; drills specific to improving movement as a whole, or focus on a segment of the movement.

j) Prepare the athlete psychologically (establish mental focus) and physically (prepare the neuromuscular and energy systems) to perform optimally within the upcoming training or competition.

The role of cool down is to:

a) Assist the athlete's body to return towards a homeostasis/resting state, by assisting with the removal of metabolic byproducts (eg, lactate), bringing the neural system back towards a resting state.

b) Should include light work of the major muscle groups to assist in the removal of metabolic byproducts.

c) Should include static stretching.

d) The type and duration of the cool down will reflect the intensity of the training session. An aerobic session cool down could be shorter than after a more intense anaerobic session, which would include a game/competition, due to the metabolites present in the athletes' bodies.

e) Adequate time must be scheduled within your program, and athletes must remain engaged in the process. If you inform athlete's of the importance of a quality cool down and what you expect to achieve, they will gain a better understanding of quality athletic behaviour for performance.

Training session design basics

No training session is viewed in isolation, but is a component of the coach's weekly/monthly/quarterly/seasonal/annual design. As an introduction, let's have a look at what a single, isolated training session might look like. For this example, let's assume it's a pre-season training session.

A standard training session design I've often seen in field/court sports tends to follow the pattern of: warm-up – fitness (running laps, sprints, planks and push-ups, etc) – drills – game play – cool down. In swimming, it tends to be: dry land warm-up – in water warm-up (perhaps building intensity, depending on main sets) – drills (sometimes included in the warm-up)– main sets – cool down.

Question: What is the fundamental difference between the two session structures above?

In the above example, swimming session overview, the fitness is incorporated into the main sets of work, whereas in the field/court sports, the fitness work is performed after the warm-up and before the more mentally demanding drills and game skills. In the skill acquisition chapter, you read how fatigue can interfere with the learning process, so why would a coach try to introduce or develop skills in fatigued athletes and expect success?

I recall some years ago watching a lacrosse training session, overhearing the coach say that he would run the players hard, then have them perform complex skills to find out who had remembered them. How valid is that? Assuming that all players are of the same skill competence, having run them hard (as a group, allowing for no individual differences) and building up varying levels of lactate depending on the athlete, which we have read can interfere with neural communication and energy availability. The coach has shown variances in anaerobic threshold (blood lactate accumulation exceeds blood lactate clearance ability) within the group, with those with a higher threshold being less affected by lactate accumulation. This would become evident during the skills section they had planned. What they have found is the individual differences in the athlete's lactate threshold based on previous work, which is a reflection of the coach's athlete development through the programming they have provided, not the athlete's ability to perform skills under a fatigued state, the latter of which they were attempting to evaluate.

The questions you must ask, include: what will be the focus – fitness, individual skills, team skills, or all of them; what level are my athletes at within their sport; how many training years have they achieved? You'll most likely want to program everything, but how realistic is that? Can you program all of these items into one session and achieve quality outcomes in all areas (or any area)? The answer is a "No". If it's early pre-season, then your training session focus should be on two main elements: specific fitness development, which includes strength development for injury prevention and performance enhancement, as well as basic sport specific-skill development. Athletes who are new or relatively new to the sport would need a different base program than those athletes who are returning for another season. This adds to the complexity for the coach, as they may need to deliver slightly different concurrent programs and ensure engagement with all athletes during the session.

The fitness development components do not involve your athletes being "hammered" into fitness (something I have often seen), but should have a strong focus on technique as well as on developing initial strength and then power in technically accurate movements.

In most land based sports, this may include teaching technical elements such as the use of mini-hurdles, fast foot ladders, drills such as "A" and "B" skips (paying particular attention to timing, foot strike, balance, hip position, posture and arm movement), first step quickness (perhaps using falling starts), agility (perhaps include star drills etc). These elements can also form a base for every warm-up. Similarly, an aquatics based sport would tend to focus on drills.

This will pay dividends as your athletes will be more efficient and correct in their movement. An increase in athlete movement efficiency will also induce less fatigue, which will result in less movement errors, better concentration and a greater ability to progressively increase workloads as the season starts.

I've already brushed on the notion of the warm-up, and to recap the warm-up should reflect the training session intensity by building into the session, and be intense enough to allow the athlete's physiology to participate fully in the session as described earlier.

It is most likely that early in the pre-season, the fitness focus you will deliver is to build a solid aerobic base. Athletes can find aerobic sessions rather boring and monotonous, and can disengage. They will still appear to do the prescribed work but are mentally disengaged, which may mean that

- Their technique quality diminishes, so they may end up performing poor quality movement repeats and learning those poor movements very well, potentially creating a "retraining" issue for you to deal with at a later time
- Their work effort lowers slightly as boredom potentially sets in. As a coach, you need to ensure ongoing engagement through quality communication with all the athletes. This should include educating them as to why the aerobic work is crucial to their overall athletic development.

I'm going to mention the importance of ensuring your athletes maintain quality technique at all times again. It's that important. Whether it's a poor foot strike in running, or a dropped wrist in swimming freestyle, as examples, you need to provide positive, corrective feedback immediately and have the athlete refocus.

If you coach a seasonal sport, then the sessions would develop from the following concepts:

- Early pre-season
- Mid pre-season
- Late pre-season
- In season
- Finals preparation (if your team makes the finals)

The above list will be discussed within the periodisation of programming section. You would use a seasonal periodised structure.

If you coach a non-seasonal sport, such as swimming, then your focus would be on the development of your athletes with the focus being on certain identified swim meets. You would use an annual periodised structure.

Task: In a seasonal sport, what would be the fundamental differences between the 5 session types outlined above?

It is not possible to describe each of the session types in detail, as sports vary; however, we can go through a broader overview of each. Below, we'll assume a seasonal program in a field/court sport.

Early pre-season:

The focus of this period is:
1. To increase physical strength
2. To build a solid aerobic foundation which will allow for future increases in intensity of work to be overlaid
3. Basic sport specific skill development (includes revisiting basic skills for more advanced athletes so that everyone is performing at the required base sport skill level you want, eg, batting, throwing, catching, running, etc)

Great care should be taken to ensure you do not ramp up any workloads too quickly, but allow time for adaptation to occur. Failure to do so may result in
- An increased injury risk
- An inability to increase work to the next programmed level
- The development and manifestation of poor technique.

The type of work you can do during the beginning stage of this element will depend on your athletes. If they are a new or a younger cohort, then you will be starting off on a low base of fitness, strength, and skills. Irrespective of age, all athletes should commence learning correct technical movement, which can take years to perfect. This should not be rushed as neural connections take time to develop. Engage your athletes by explaining to them the reason why they are doing drills that seem removed from actually playing the game. Younger athletes often cannot relate the efficiency of movement you are trying to teach to the game, as they'd rather be kicking or hitting a ball around.

Aerobic foundation work is performed at an easy pace, over an extended period during a session, with recovery time allowed. As a note, the recovery time required is short, as no lactate should have accumulated beyond the athletes rate of lactate clearance. An indicator of aerobic work would be that athlete's will be able to engage in light conversation. Light efforts may involve running for several blocks of 10 minutes plus in duration – this will depend on the age and athletic background of your athletes. Aerobic fitness takes months to manifest, so it will form a part of all training sessions, whether it's aerobic development or aerobic maintenance.

As an example during my time as the swim/sprints coach for water polo scholarship athletes at a sports institute (example aerobic and anaerobic programs are in Appendix 2), to demonstrate the positive effect aerobic work can have on repeated sprint performance. After initial technical swim assessments, they performed a sprint test (12 x 25 metre maximum effort, push start, 5 seconds rest each 25 metre), followed by 6 weeks of aerobic training (with much athlete complaint revolving around the relevance of long distance – albeit with programmed increasing aerobic intensity week on week), followed by another sprint test. All athletes performed better on the subsequent sprint test. In essence, by increasing their aerobic threshold, they were able to sustain a higher repeat speed, as was evidenced by an overall flatter slope of the curve of the graphed 25 metre times and lower cumulative time for the whole test set. The athletes trained with me three times per week, as well as gym work, and water polo-specific training.

Because the athletes are not accumulating lactate during aerobic work beyond the athletes' lactate removal rate, it would be reasonable to engage in skills work as well, after ensuring full recovery. An alternate could be to have a session structure such as: warm-up – skills – aerobic training- cool down. It is worth noting that, as the body stresses are very low, the warm-up and cool down would be low intensity.

During this phase, there is no need to cycle the in-weekly sessions in intensity (eg, medium-hard-easy), as overload is highly unlikely due to the general low intensity and minimal intensity increases.

Mid Pre-season

The focus is very similar to the early pre-season, with the main difference being the introduction of game-play.

The aerobic fitness development continues as you are still trying to raise the athlete's aerobic threshold. Changes in the aerobic threshold (the inflection point where lactate accumulation exceeds lactate removal) take at least 6 weeks of aerobic-specific training, training at least three times per week. This work is split over the early and mid pre-season programming. Your program would show a gradual ramp-up of aerobic work during this period. The emphasis is on 'gradual' ramping – ramp up the workload too quickly and your athletes will not have the time to physiologically adapt, and you also run the risk of pushing into the anaerobic training space too early, before the aerobic base has been sufficiently developed.

The advantage of aerobic work is that the athletes require very little recovery time between workout sets for each session and between training days.

As you are not driving the athletes hard (programming that produces residual lactate), you will have a higher likelihood of success at introducing new motor skills, which will include individual movement skills such as catching, hitting, running, etc, as well as group skills, which include basic game play drills, etc.

This will allow you to program each training session in what is often described as follows:
- Introduce the session goals
- Dynamic warm-up, including sport-specific drills (running drills, swimming drills)
- Sport-specific individual skills (catching, throwing, dribbling, etc), allowing time for individual instruction
- Aerobic sets (providing individual feedback to develop technique efficiency)
- Team-based skills (team drills/plays) You must be very careful to control the intensity during this section of your session program, as often athletes will want to work harder than you desire, thereby building lactate, which will potentially interfere with new skill

development/motor learning, as well as require a modification to your cool down protocol to remove the lactate.

- Light cool down

As your athletes have not produced residual lactate, the cool down can be short if required.

A review of your session programs to date should show a very gradual but continuous increase in intensity of aerobic work week-on-week, with the last 7-10 days approaching the aerobic threshold for the individual athletes. There will be some variance between athletes, but with experience, you will be able to program the correct workloads at an individual athlete level if desired.

Late Pre-season

In an ideal world, I would hope to be able to allocate 4-5 weeks to this section of training. Due to the increase in training loading during the sessions, the warm-up will be longer and build to a higher intensity than for the purely aerobic training sessions. The athletes must be in a state of light sweat after the warm-up. The primary 'fitness' focus during this period is to develop anaerobic tolerance, train towards achieving game/race speed/endurance/repeat sprint ability by the end. The sport-specific and team-based skill development should be at or over competition pace. The cool down will be considerably longer in duration.

There are several key points that set these training sessions apart from the early and mid-season training sessions:

- Warm-up ends at a higher intensity than in previous training sessions; at the end of the warm-up, the athletes are slightly sweaty
- No (or at best very limited) new skills are introduced, as the efficacy of teaching will be diminished
- The athletes will cover less distance due to the efforts and longer recovery time required
- The recovery between efforts must be programmed and timed to ensure recovery to a pre-determined level to allow for the required repeat efforts
- This work will have best success if you have built your athletes' aerobic base first
- Cool down will be much longer and it will be more of an active cool-down, as you want to remove as much residual lactate as possible. A cool-down of fifteen minutes plus would not be inappropriate

As a new coach, it may be difficult to determine how recovered an athlete is after each repeat or set of work. You can use how they talk as a guide, whether conversation is easy (aerobic), a few words at a time (threshold/anaerobic), or can't get a single word out (maximal anaerobic effort). In the latter two cases, have your athletes keep gently moving, as this will assist in lactate removal, unless your goal is to increase lactate to very high levels, which is not likely with new or newer athletes. You may also notice a reddening of the athletes skin, particularly the face, as well as on the upper chest and upper back, which is a result of secondary anaerobic programming effect redistributing the blood supply nearer the skin.

If your athletes' lactate levels increase to very high levels, then they may feel nauseous and possibly vomit. Their heart rate may also go very high, perhaps over 200 beats/minute.

In Season

If you're coaching a seasonal sport, then the goals during this period (other than winning games, of course) are to maintain the athletes' fitness and skill levels. Once the season commences, your athletes will have an additional training session performed at competition level intensity each week, in addition to the preexisting training sessions. I'm referring to the game day match itself. Some coaches may already have programmed the normal match day as a training session late in the pre-season training program to be able to simulate a normal in-season week. Key considerations for the coach during the competition season include:

- Allowing for recovery from the game day
- Having flexibility in session programming to allow for a less-than optimal post-game day recovery (if the game/match was particularly hard, to modify the intended training session program to reflect this).
- Not to load lactate into the athlete's system without ensuring removal in preparation for the next game/match.
- Not allow aerobic or anaerobic fitness to diminish.
- Allow for psychological recovery as well as for physical recovery.
- Manage and understand acute injuries sustained during the game/match (knocks, sprains, etc)
- Continue to develop/rehearse game plays.

If you're coaching a year round sport with occasional competitions, such as swimming, then your programming will tend to follow a repeated cycle of aerobic conditioning – threshold – anaerobic – taper, spread over a 6-10 week time frame, sometimes training hard through a competition to focus and prepare for an identified and targeted competition.

Finals Preparation

Finals preparation commences several weeks out from the actual finals series, depending on where your team is on the table. If you are nearer the top, then you are more likely to be playing in the finals, and your finals-specific training can commence earlier than if you're team only has a marginal chance of playing finals.

If your team falls into the latter category, then your training should follow the same in-season format, as you don't want to unnecessarily ramp up your athletes training which will leave them fatigued and less able to perform physically and psychologically, thereby limiting your chances of playing finals.

If your team is highly likely to play finals, then you can think about ramping up their fitness during training sessions in a controlled manner. If you go too hard, the risk of injury increases, as does the risk of chronic fatigue setting in (your athletes may already be showing signs of fatigue, particularly if the season has been long). You want to arrive at a position where your athletes have improved in required fitness and are fresh, so as to be able to successfully compete.

The key takeaway is that you cannot find or generate large improvements in the last few weeks of a season. This is a culmination of all of your seasonal incremental programming. At this point, slight tweaking at the edges, continuing to work on your athlete's resilience and confidence, your team's cohesiveness, as well as their fitness maintenance, should be your focus.

Periodisation of programming

It is critical that, as a coach, you develop a training program that supports a multi-year training (MYT) model, which engineers a controlled incremental approach to athletic development covering their complete junior years. A MYT plan allows for adaptation to occur, thereby minimising mal-adaptation risk while maximising athletic development over the long term.

If you only have the athletes for that season (which can be the case in age group sports), your program should build upon the previous year's program and deliver in the current year the designed incremental developments. Your program structure in a seasonal sport should have structural components of a pre-season section and an in-season/competition section as a minimum. Year-round sports, such as swimming, require a different structure to the seasonal sports plan, which would focus on athlete preparation towards specific competitions within a periodised cycle over the year. This structure is further broken down into more refined segments, such as physiological development (aerobic, anaerobic, lactate tolerance, ATP/CP), strength development, power development, speed work, endurance work, etc. These segments would represent blocks of work appropriate to meet your goals over time, and would be progressive. For example, strength work precedes power work, as power represents the functional application of the strength gained.

154

Once the structure with it's segments have been developed and written down (I used the annual calendar at the front of a yearly diary to indicate in general terms what the work focus would be during a specific period), then you can write the daily training programs on the "day" page in the diary that will support and deliver the desired programmed segment outcomes. This will allow you to add post-program delivery notes and provide a record of annual programs.

Basic Examples:

Year-round ongoing program.

Let's decide that our programming will be based on a 6-week cycle. Firstly, divide the year into 6-week sections. We'll assume there will be 48 weeks in your year, allowing for holidays, which will provide you with 8 x 6-week cycles. You then make a decision on how many weeks to devote to each physiological stress. You decide the cycle will be structured as: 3 weeks aerobic, 1.5 weeks threshold, 1 week anaerobic, the rest of the days are a taper/recovery.

Alternatively, you may decide on 6 blocks of 8 weeks, with a structure of: 4 weeks aerobic, 1.5 weeks threshold, 1.5 week anaerobic, 0.5 weeks ATP/CP, the rest of the block is taper/recovery.

In the above blocks, the aerobic work gradually ramps up week on week towards threshold pace/efforts, which then ramps towards anaerobic work. To the athlete, it should appear as a continuous and seamless increase in workload, with the volume of work done reducing as the rest periods (recovery) between repetitions/sets increase, with a corresponding increase in the work intensity.

A strength and conditioning structure may be based upon a 3 or 4 week cycle, with, for example, in a 4 week block: 2.5 weeks of strength work, 1 week of functional power work, followed by a taper to allow for supercompensation.

In my water polo work, I used a 12-week cycle, as that was the best fit for the national competition program, with it's 12-week competition season. I broke the 12-week training blocks into: 6 weeks aerobic, 3 weeks threshold, 2 weeks anaerobic ATP/CP, 1 week recovery, with testing at the end of the recovery week. This gave me 3x12 week training blocks plus a 12 week playing season and a 4 week post-season break.

Each block is written in your calendar, identifying the weekly workload type. From that, you then write each daily session/s based on the required loading to deliver. After each training session, you write down notes as to the effectiveness of the programmed session. You then use the training workloads with your notes to design the following weeks sessions, following your yearly program design. Further to the "fitness" training design and notes, you also write down the skills development you intend to focus on.

The skills development programming should be designed to ensure that you teach the movement/skill/drill/play, taking into account an understanding of the precedence of movement (and the kinetic chain of movement). In that way, your teaching programming will not leave out a fundamental step. You also need to remember the negative effects anaerobic work and fatigue have on skill acquisition when programming skill elements within your segments.

A review of each session is very important, as is a weekly review of your training prescription. As a coach, you should always be prepared to accept your critical review and modify your design to ensure a cohesive and appropriate program.

Irrespective of your written-down program, it would be unwise to stubbornly stick with it at all costs if you notice that it is not effective, or that your athletes are becoming bored or are showing signs of excess fatigue when you should not be expecting excess fatigue to be evident. You may also find that your athletes (some or all) attend a training session showing obvious signs of fatigue on that day, due to perhaps a mentally or physically demanding day at school/university/work, in which case a change to your session program could be prudent. This ad hoc change to your program should also involve a reassessment of any skills work you were planning, as it is less likely to be effective.

You should not be too concerned if you need to instigate a change to your program. A one-off training session change will not make much difference to outcomes when viewed over the season. A more significant rewrite of the broader training period or even the year's design should be seen as a learning opportunity and not as a failure on your part. To be able to analyse the athlete's performance against your outcome expectations and determine that there is an inconsistency which you will address through modification and adjustment to your program shows your level of awareness and confidence in accepting that your athlete's outcomes rest in great part on your program design.

Adaptation

As your athletes perform the work that you have programmed within your periodised structure, they should adapt to the workloads prescribed over time. Time is the critical element within the adaptation process. If you try to achieve performance improvements in a rushed or poorly controlled manner, then your athletes may not be able to physically adapt to the workloads before your ramp up workloads again, which could lead to catastrophic physical and/or psychological outcomes and mal-adaptation.

A key to allowing for adaptation to occur is for you to have a written-out, carefully constructed training plan, broken down into controlled sections of rising applied stress, such as:
- Pre-season (early, mid, late) – in-season – mid-season break – in-season – finals, or perhaps
- Aerobic base – aerobic threshold – anaerobic – taper, or perhaps
- Strength – functional power – super-compensation (taper)

The notion of "rising applied stress" should not be considered as a straight line continuum, but rather as a jagged line of varying stress levels with a slight incline. You need to allow the athletes various metabolic systems and functional structures to adapt to the workloads before ramping up. As an example, if you choose to program plyometrics, then you do need to ensure that the athlete has developed the required strength in advance to be able to perform the plyometrics safely. As another example, if you program the athlete to perform squats with a bar (plus weights), you need to ensure that enough preparatory strength work, including form development, has occurred to avoid injury and maximise results.

Overload

To generate athletic improvement, as a coach, you need to provide a measured and controlled increase in the stimulus you provide to the athlete to elicit a physiologic response from the system you are stressing. Overloading muscles will stimulate the production of new proteins; increase capillary development in the affected muscles; improve neural-muscular recruitment efficacy; improve the circulatory system to be better able to provide oxygen and remove waste products from the working muscles.

The variables available to the coach are:
- Frequency (how often) – sessions/week/per month/per year/per periodised cycle
- Intensity (workload) – training load per day/week/month/year/periodised cycle
- Time (duration of stress/stimulus) – hours per day/week/month/year/periodised cycle
- Recovery – time allowed for the athlete to adapt to the overload stress

However, if you do not apply an appropriate stimulus stress to the system you wish to improve, improvement will either be less than expected or will not occur at all. (The workload stress you apply may however, improve a physiologic area you are not measuring) Too high stressors can lead to injury, over-training or mal-adaptation to occur. As a coach, you are looking for the

"Goldilocks" zone, where just the right amount of system stress is applied to elicit the desired response, not too little nor too much.

The change in the variables to create an overload situation could include:
- In strength training – increasing the amount of weight, increasing the repetitions, increasing the time muscles are under load by slowing the movement
- In endurance running-based sports – increase the running time, increase the intensity (either by increasing the tempo or introducing a very slight incline, for example)

Some simple signs for the coach to be aware of and to consider:
- The notion of "No pain, No gain" is a nonsense which snuck out of the old school locker room under the cover of darkness and still circulates around today. Athletes should not be in pain. Athletes should suffer from discomfort if the programming dictates it. That is profoundly different from pain. I always let my athletes know what level of discomfort (sometimes their expected heart rate zones as well) that they should expect in the day's program, if they performed the program as expected. This was a way for them to 'self-check' to ensure the stress applied was appropriate.
- You have to break down muscle to gain muscular improvement. The breaking down of muscle involves muscle trauma through micro-tearing, which causes oedema, which causes pain, and requires the athlete to rest to allow for the muscle repair to occur. (There are caveats to this, as there are situations where you want to cause muscle micro-damage, but that is high-level specialised

coaching and not something the new/newer coach should consider)

- Lactic acid causes muscle soreness – no. Lactic acid is metabolised soon after exercise, but the soreness often referred to as occurring due to lactic acid buildup remains for 24-48 hours afterwards. The pain is due to micro-trauma to the muscles and connective tissue (this involves not only oedema but also enzyme involvement, but that discussion is outside the scope of this book).

If you are involved in a sport where the athletes only train during the season and have a lengthy off-season, you will notice that when they come back, they will have lost many attributes, including: fitness (in all its forms), speed, technical skills, muscle atrophy (reduction in muscle cross-sectional area) etc. This is as a result of regression. It occurs because the systems are no longer stressed to appropriate levels, and there has been no persistence in training stressors. Persistence of training stressors cannot be underestimated.

If we accept that an athlete must be trained within a periodised program to be able to manage stressors in a controlled and progressive way, that over training (too much too soon, ramping up workloads too quickly) can lead to illness or injury, which in turn prevents the athlete from training, which leads to regression, then perhaps the coach can conclude that an off-season training plan could be beneficial and form a part of your annual periodised plan.

Progression

The controlled progressive programming of training supports the requirements of work overload by allowing time for recovery and adaptation. It should also be accepted that progressive improvements do not follow a continuum to infinity, but rather have a ceiling for each athlete.

Athletic progression involves specificity of training, which follows next. As a coach, you need to be aware that although you are providing a thought-out progression of specific training, your athlete's progress may stall. This is normal. It is referred to as a 'consolidation' phase. It can occur when the athlete needs to assemble many varying parts or skills into a cohesive movement and broader ability. The problem occurs when the consolidation phase appears stuck. It's difficult to put an absolute time frame on how long is too long, but a frank discussion with your athlete is critical. As a coach, you need a plan of action to assist the athlete to again be able to improve. This shouldn't be an issue with new/newer athletes, but with longer-standing athletes it may be. Depending on where the athlete is in their development, a three-month or even a 1 year consolidation time may not be beyond reason, if supported by evidence and a plan.

Specificity

Simply put, the training stimulus you provide will yield specific results related to that stimulus. The concept of specificity relates to the energy systems, muscular development, neural recruitment, and movement patterns involved in the activity.

To train as a swimmer, you don't practice running. If you are training sprint runners, they don't do marathon runs. It seems obvious that these activities are not compatible. If you train your athletes in a structure of activities that are not compatible with the sport, they will not achieve the outcomes you or they desire. You will most likely become frustrated, the athletes will most likely become frustrated, you will not achieve what you have set out to achieve, nor will the athletes, who will also likely leave or not return for the following season.

As a coach, you need to determine the energy systems your athletes utilise to perform. You need to understand the endurance they need, the repeat sprint ability they require. You need to understand the movements involved for the athlete to be able to execute those movements efficiently and correctly.

> Question: How well do you know and understand the discrete movements your athletes need to be able to perform?

There is a profound difference between performing a task/movement as an athlete and teaching a task/movement as a coach. As a coach, you need to be able to break down any movement into it's component parts, from the proximal to distal, from the whole movement to each distinct segment, and know how the movement (or part of the movement) within one segment can affect another segment within the movement sequence (the kinetic chain). Without that understanding, you may find it quite difficult to determine where your intervention should focus and may inadvertently provide correction of the movement, which either exacerbates the problem or creates new ones.

Further information is contained in the chapter on skill acquisition.

Variation of work

It is simple for a coach to have a set of training sessions that they keep recycling (and surprisingly expect different results!). It demonstrates that the coach is not reviewing and improving the programming they provide. At a more basic level, if we assume that the programs are providing the appropriate stimulus to the athlete, it nevertheless may lead to boredom of the athletes due to the repetitive and predictable nature of the programming. This is more likely to be the case with junior athletes, leading to a lowering of engagement, diminished performance outcomes and potentially an increase in drop out rate. The challenge for the coach is to design novel programs that deliver the same specific stimulus.

To vary the type of work and achieve the same physiologic result can be challenging and may not be possible beyond slight 'tweaks'.

As an example, when I was delivering a fitness/running program in a newly created under 17 boys high performance lacrosse program (see Appendix 1 for the program), I shifted from an oval which focused on aerobic work as well as technical running/first step acceleration skills to the beach for sand work (a short 20 metre long section) which tied in with the anaerobic training cycle. (The athletes enjoyed the warm-up, until they realised I had them simply 'fluff' up the sand to make it very loose with very little traction for the main work sets). The stimulation of using a different training environment with the athletes was very high, further increasing engagement.

Many sports require agility, so introduce agility drills, such as star drills, evasion belts etc. Modify the drills to incorporate game elements. Time the athletes (even if you keep the times to yourself, as another measure of your program efficacy). Introduce a distraction into the work. Play another sport, for example, for netball/basketball/hockey etc, why not play flag football in a small grassed space? The athlete will work on their agility, teamwork, first step quickness, anaerobic system, neural system, vision, etc. This could be done after warm-up and sport-specific skills work. As a swim coach, once or twice a year I'd get out a water polo ball near the end of a session. It's surprising how they can tread water without complaint for ages when they are playing a game. Modify the 'game' so that all players without the ball must keep one hand on their head to increase the intensity of the workload. Keep training interesting, and the athletes will keep interested, especially with new/newer athletes.

Aerobic Training

Aerobic training (defined as slow to moderate intensity work) of an athlete leads to an improvement in their endurance capacity, which allows the athlete to sustain prolonged exercise. The aerobic (chemical process with oxygen) system uses carbohydrates and fat as its main energy sources to produce energy.

Two elements should be noted here. The change or adaptations by muscles are in response to both the level of exercise intensity, exercise session duration, and the length (number of sessions/weeks) of the training program's exposure to aerobic work.

Question: Do you need to aerobically train your athletes if you sport only requires short-duration "burst type" intensity work?

The short answer to the above question is "yes". Let's look at an overview of why that would be the case.

For an athlete to maintain a high speed requires a single muscle or muscle group to sustain a high intensity, repetitive movement/s, and/or static holds, then the athlete requires muscular endurance. In turn, muscular endurance is strongly related to muscular strength and anaerobic development/performance.

If we broaden our view to a "whole of body" perspective, we can say that aerobic development relates to the development of the cardio-vascular and respiratory systems.

To combine these two thoughts, aerobic training develops two "physiologies": muscular endurance and cardio-respiratory endurance.

Aerobic training effects and muscular endurance

In general terms, repeated use of muscles stimulates changes within those muscle fibres in various ways. This can include energy availability, cross-sectional area, increased capillary density, increased efficiency in available energy use, and increased intramuscular energy availability.

Muscles are made of two types of fibres – slow twitch (ST) and two variants of fast twitch fibres (Fta and Ftb). For simplicity, I will refer to FTa and FTb as a collective FT, ignoring their differences.

The effects of aerobic training on ST fibres include:
- ST fibre bundles become larger due to an increase in their cross-sectional area.
- An increase in the number of blood capillaries surrounding each muscle fibre allows for a greater exchange of gases, heat and nutrients, as well as an increase in the diffusion of oxygen to the mitochondria (mitochondria are the cells aerobic energy producing engine, therefore by extension, the more oxygen that is available the more work is possible) This change (an increase in mitochondrial density/cell) begins to manifest after several weeks of appropriate aerobic training.
- ST fibres are red due to their myoglobin content. The iron-rich myoglobin shuttles the oxygen molecules from the cell membrane to the mitochondria. Aerobic training increases muscular myoglobin content.

Other effects of aerobic training include:
- An increase in mitochondria size and density.
- An increase in mitochondrial efficiency, through changes in oxidative enzyme activity which is thought to improve the athletes ability to sustain a higher intensity of work for longer. The reason is an increase in the lactate threshold.
- An increased capacity for the athlete to utilise fat as a fuel source, which in turn increases maximal endurance capacity.
- An increase in blood plasma volume.
- Decrease in resting heart rate.
- Lower heart rate for the same sub-maximal work.
- Increase in cardiac stroke volume.

- Post effort heart rate recovery back to resting level is achieved more quickly.
- An increase in red blood cell count.

Lactate threshold. You've probably heard of this term, but what is it?

Definition: The lactate threshold is when, during exercise of increasing intensity, blood lactate levels increase to a point where lactate clearance is no longer able to keep up with lactate accumulation. This is the point where the aerobic energy system cannot supply all the energy required.

Definition: Lactate is a salt of lactic acid. As lactic acid dissociates, it causes an accumulation of hydrogen ions (H^+), resulting in muscle acidification, known as acidosis. Using this concept, lactate in itself is not an inhibitor of performance; however, the acidosis is, as the change in blood pH caused by the H^+ interferes with various processes. To recap from earlier, all energy systems are working at the same time, however, depending on the type of work (intensity, duration) it determines which energy system is emphasised, with associated metabolic stressors and changes.

If all energy systems are in simultaneous operation at all times, the assumption is made that lactic acid is always being produced via the anaerobic system and dissociates, liberating H^+ ions. To counter the H^+ production, cells contain buffers to "mop" up the ions in the form of bicarbonate. The anaerobic threshold is reached when the buffers within the blood and cells can no longer "mop up" the H^+. which then leads to the lowering of blood pH. (For your interest, the measure taken is how many mmol/L lactic acid is present. The threshold point is around 4 mmol/L)

The acidosis, which occurs once the buffers are overwhelmed, effect both energy production and muscle contraction, limiting performance and leading to fatigue.

From the above chain of events, it would be ideal to be able to move the lactate threshold "up" so that more work could be performed by the athlete at a higher intensity and duration before the effects of acidosis take effect on performance.

The lactate threshold point increases with endurance (aerobic) training, allowing the athlete to perform at higher rates of work, utilising higher levels of oxygen consumption without increasing blood lactate levels. It can also increase the athlete's blood lactate tolerance. To summarise, the athlete can exercise at a higher intensity for a longer period by predominantly using their aerobic energy system, facilitated by effective aerobic programming.

Anaerobic training effects

Work that focuses on the anaerobic energy system (also known as anaerobic glycolysis, may also be abbreviated to An+) is usually referred to as "sprint" work, that is, work of a high intensity and short time duration.

The term high intensity is self-explanatory (the athlete cannot hold a conversation at best, they can communicate using only a word or two at a time), with the exercise time duration being less than five minutes at most. In essence, the anaerobic energy system usage focus refers to sprinting activities, either as a one-off sprint (eg 100 metre sprint) or repeated short sprints (as in field or court sports, water polo, gymnastic routines, etc).

The anaerobic energy system is the dominant energy system when the athlete commences exercise, increases their pace or engages in high-intensity efforts such as engaging in short burst maximal sprint efforts during a game or a final burst effort at the end of a predominant endurance event (such as a 10,000 metre run).

As a coach, it is almost certain that you will want to program time to stress/develop the anaerobic energy system.

Anaerobic Glycolysis

Let's briefly (and simply) review what anaerobic glycolysis is about. You've already read about the aerobic energy system that produces energy from the breakdown of carbohydrates and fat with the use of oxygen. In contrast, the anaerobic energy system produces energy from carbohydrate (not fats) without the use of oxygen.

Using a simplistic straight timeline of energy system usage, the athlete will commence with the very short-lived adenosine triphosphate (ATP) and phosphocreatine (PCr) energy system, which lasts for only a few seconds. This is followed by a predominant reliance on the anaerobic energy system for the next 3-5 minutes of work, followed by the aerobic energy system becoming the dominant energy system thereafter. This represents a simplistic timeline which should help you, as a new/newer coach, to have a workable overview.

It is worth noting that the time delay for the aerobic energy system to "kick in" is due to the time taken for the chemistry-driven processes to commence.

In the aerobic energy system section we discussed the accumulation of H+ ions in the blood stream due to the athlete engaging in anaerobic efforts. H+ ions alter the acid balance to allow an accumulation of lactate in the muscle fibres, which affects the muscle fibres' ability to perform by: interfering with the aerobic energy production pathway, and reducing enzyme activity; reducing muscle contraction forces; causing physical performance decline and an increase in mental fatigue (affecting decision making, motivation, etc).

With that in mind, and referring back to the aerobic section, the deleterious effects of lactate accumulation beyond the capacity for the athlete to remove the lactate with its associated effect on limiting performance, highlights the need in your programming to allow for the development of a sound aerobic system to increase the aerobic threshold (amount of work the athlete can perform aerobically before lactate accumulation affects performance).

To recap, many sports require the athlete to engage in a maximal all-out effort (eg, running a sprint race or a swim sprint), or repeated high-intensity efforts with short breaks in between (eg, field and court sports, water polo).

We know that the energy utilised for maximal all-out efforts is provided by the anaerobic energy system, in what is referred to as anaerobic power, which provides energy for a few seconds before anaerobic glycolysis becomes the primary energy source for the next few minutes.

As a coach, you are now aware that when the athlete's energy requirements for their performance is derived form anaerobic glycolysis (to remind – energy derived without oxygen involved), the byproduct of lactic acid is produced which causes acidosis of the blood, measured in mmol/L which can interfere with muscle contraction, power, coordination and decision making, thereby reducing the athletes performance potential.

The basic information concerning lactic acid blood levels is presented in this book to give you a superficial understanding to be able to develop successful training programs, why you should most likely include aerobic and anaerobic programming, and to give you the ability to understand any articles you may come across that involve discussion of blood lactate levels in athletic performance. As a new/newer coach you won't have access to blood lactate measuring equipment (although it is relatively cheap now and easily accessible), I contend you don't need this equipment unless you're involved with sub-elite or higher athletes.

Question: Why can some athletes cope with a higher workload intensity with less performance impairment than other athletes?

The answer to the above relates to "lactate threshold". The same work-load may elicit different lactate impact in different athletes, potentially due to individual variances in lactate threshold because of their training background and their response to that training.

An athlete's lactate threshold is reached when the increasing lactate accumulation in the blood can no longer be removed at the same rate as the accumulation. In other words, lactic acid levels rise and continue to do so with a noticeable impact on performance.

The rise in lactate begins at the commencement of exercise. During easy workloads, blood lactate levels increase from a resting level of 1mmol/L to 2mmol/L (sometimes referred to as the LT1 inflection point). With increasing intensity beyond LT1, lactate levels rise faster towards a second inflection point (LT2) where the blood lactate levels are about 4mmol/L. Lactate levels can go very high with increasing intensity, up to 20mmol/L. Swimming coaches use the LT2 inflection point (4mmol/L) in their interval training to determine the individual optimal race pace. Training at the LT2 point provides performance gains.

Back to our last question. The answer is not clear-cut, with individual athletes performing differently (with a rate of blood lactate increase) due to the following factors:
- Motivation – some athletes will work to the expected intensity, others may not. Some may also work too hard, thereby ramping up too quickly.
- Individual tolerance levels to being 'uncomfortable' vary between athletes, which can limit how hard they work.
- Individual response/sensitivity to training loads (*see next paragraph).
- Prepubescent/post-pubescent differences. Prepubescent athletes have an immature anaerobic energy system, so they don't tend to accumulate lactic acid to a significant level.

* You will find that there will be a difference in the physiologic response between athletes to the same training program. Some athletes will be 'non-responders' (they show minimal or less than

expected gains) while others are 'responders' (they show maximal gains).

Adaptations to anaerobic training

- Anaerobic training (sprint and resistance training) is carried out at high intensities with short durations, and predominantly recruits fast-twitch muscle fibres, which, over time, in response to the training stress, increase in cross-sectional area.
- Short burst (less than 5 seconds) sprints have been shown to increase muscular strength.
- Improvement in efficiency of movement, through the optimisation of muscle fibre recruitment, leading to movement efficiency gains.
- Increase in blood buffering capacity (*see next paragraph).
- Anaerobic training (eg, repeated 30-second maximal sprints) also increases the muscle's aerobic capacity, increasing the time to fatigue by enhancing aerobic metabolism and reducing anaerobic ATP generation.

* Blood buffers (for example, bicarbonate) combine with the H+ ions in the blood, thereby reducing blood acidity, which in turn delays fatigue onset during anaerobic work. The blood buffering capacity can increase by between 12% and 50% following eight weeks of anaerobic training.

The reason that you need to be familiar with both anaerobic and aerobic energy systems and how they impede/support athlete performance, is that you can determine the importance of the energy systems within your sport (or different energy system requirements dependant on field position), and how to stress the energy systems appropriately to achieve your desired outcomes through the development and delivery of effective training programming.

Training Diary Structure Examples

Example of setting up your training diary for a seasonal field-based sport. For example, I'll assume a nine-week pre-season (3 weeks each of early, mid, and late pre-season), followed by a seven-week first-season half, a two week break, a seven week second-half season, followed by a finals series.

	Pre-Season			In-Season			Finals
	Early 1-3	Mid 4-6	Late 7-9	1st Half	Break	2nd Half	
Physiology:	Aerobic base	Aerobic base to threshold	Aerobic base anaerobic	Game intensity; Game recovery	aerobic maintenance	Game intensity; Game recovery	
Skills:	Basic development	Early game play skills	Game play skills	Game plays etc	New game skills identified	Game plays etc	

176

These broad items are written on the annual planner page of your coach's diary.
*Physiology refers to the primary focus of training efforts
*Skills- these will vary depending upon the preexisting skill level your athletes present with

Let's extend out the early pre-season section.

Early Pre-Season		
Week 1	Week 2	Week 3
Base aerobic Base strength Basic skills	Base aerobic Base strength Basic skills	Base aerobic Base strength Base sprint technique Basic skills

Now let's extend our week 1. We'll assume three training sessions per week, allowing 1.5-2 hours per training session.

	Week 1					
Monday Session 1	Tuesday	Wednesday Session 2	Thursday	Friday Session 3	Saturday	Sunday
Program: aerobic-warm-up; skills; aerobic game play; strength; cool down	Rest	Program: same structure as session 1	Rest	Program: same structure as session 1	Rest	Rest

178

Note that there are four "rest" days. These are days when the athlete does not have formal training; however, it is deceptive to call them a "rest" day. On these days you can prescribe light work to the athletes, such as continuing to do strength work (eg lateral and prone planks, push-ups, sit-ups etc), proprioception and balance work (eg stand on one leg, eyes closed and touch your nose, etc); skills work (eg wall ball, dribbling etc), stretching work.

Now that you have determined the session structure, you will fill in the work the athletes will do to fulfil the requirements of each session program heading. This is written on the relevant day in your coaching diary. I used a spreadsheet to assist in this process, which calculated the time durations of each repetition and set, rest periods, etc, to provide accurate timing for the session program.

After each training session, you then write notes on that page as to the overall efficacy and cohesiveness of the training session, and use that information to help guide the development of the next training session. Having a record of the actual work the athletes have performed allows you to accurately control the ramping up of intensities of effort and strength work, and later the intensities of power/sprint work.

Just as a point of comparison, let's generate an example of week 9 of the pre-season (late pre-season).

			Week 9				
Monday Session 1	Tuesday	Wednesday Session 2	Thursday	Friday Session 3	Saturday	Sunday
Program: warm-up to a high intensity; skills at high intensity; power sprint work; game pace plays; plyometrics; long cool down	Rest	Program: same structure as week 9, session 1	Rest	Program: same structure as week 9, session 1	Rest	Rest

Although the training sessions comparing weeks 1 and 9 are of the same time duration, the distances covered during week 9 will be considerably less than the distances covered in week 1. From the explanations in the sections detailing the differences between aerobic and anaerobic energy systems, it is clear that the higher the workload, the greater the rest periods between each set or work items to allow for recovery, so the correct physiology remains the focus of the exercise stress.

Not allowing for adequate recovery within and between training sets will not produce the training benefits you are expecting. It is likely to interfere with learning skills, is demotivating, and can lead to a greater risk of injury.

To close this example, let's develop a week program for during the playing season, assuming a Saturday game. I have moved the Friday training session to Thursday, as you would not tend to have a training session the day before a game.

Week 12

Monday Session 1	Tuesday	Wednesday Session 2	Thursday Session 3	Friday	Saturday	Sunday
Program: aerobic warm-up; skills and drills; game drills; game plays; aerobic maintenance; cool down	Rest	Program: moderate intensity warm-up; skills and drills; game plays; game plays at intensity; sprint work; cool down	Program: moderate intensity warm-up; skills and drills; game plays/tactics for upcoming game; cool down	Rest	Program: Game day intensity warm-up; quality post-match cool down	Rest

182

All session warm-ups would include running drills (if it's a running-based sport), such as A and B skips; mini-hurdle work, fast foot ladders, 20 metre sprint run-throughs, agility poles, perhaps easy plyometrics, etc. This includes the session 1 aerobic warm-up, where the sprint work (which would be a minor focus) would occur after the aerobic warm-up. The sport-specific skills, drills, and game drills would include elements identified as weaknesses or 'works in progress' during the game. The game drills on Monday are segments of game plays that were identified as problematic during the game. The rest days would still require the athlete to continue looking after their recovery.

You need to remember that a game against an opponent for points is considerably different from an internal trial game. The game stress on the players can yield a significant difference in how well they perform skills. As an example, during a game, players under stress will find that their peripheral vision reduces, which manifests in them not being able to 'see' opportunities or threats that appear obvious to other players and from those on the sidelines. This is just something to keep in mind when you are analysing the game and player performances.

Time to go and coach

This book should have provided you with the basic tools to be able to become a more effective and confident coach. However, this should only be the commencement of your own continuous learning program. What you do in your coaching today will most likely be modified, if not actually changed in the future. To remain effective and relevant into the future you should always be open to identifying and evaluating new concepts, be critical in their review, and not succumb to confirmation bias.

A word of caution. Don't be too eager to jump onto the latest 'trend'. I've seen many trends come and go over the years, with most being ineffective at best. Take time to critically evaluate the trend, instead of blindly following the 'herd', take your time. Many trends found on the internet are short-lived and have little benefit to your athlete's outcomes, and may in fact cause harm. Always consider the motivation behind the content creator of your internet-based information and what they have actually achieved with their idea within a science-based approach to evaluation. There is no 'quick fix' or 'magic formula' for developing your athletes.

There are several key things to remember:
- Why you started coaching in the first place. Was it to give back to the sport you love, or to develop athletes and have them enjoy the sport as you did when you competed?
- Why the athletes are there, attending every training session and competition.

- Maintain a professional distance and attitude between yourself and the athletes. You are their coach, not their friend.
- Show resilience and toughness, but also compassion when required.
- Be organised, be informed, show leadership.
- Don't shy away from difficult discussions/situations. Always maintain emotional control.
- Enjoy your time coaching, it will be contagious.

Identify people whom you can ask questions of to assist you in your learning and development. People who have coached for a long time have also most likely come across many of the concerns or issues you may have, and may be able to provide you with guidance or information. It takes courage to do, it is a sign of both strength and conviction – aren't these some of the qualities you want in your athletes too?

If you work with junior athletes, you will most likely find that what you say and do will have a profound effect on them. A poorly chosen word or phrase can undo many months of relationship development.

Junior athletes and their parents/caregivers entrust you to look after their best interests. This can be seen as a great responsibility, as you will be a part of the junior athletes' physical, emotional, and social development.

Although coaching is complex and demanding, it can be the most enjoyable and rewarding activity you will ever be involved in.

Appendix 1

Sand Running Programming

Under 17 male.

Cone sets-up: 10 mtr, 15 mtr, 20 mtr, 25mtr, 30 mtr, 35mtr.

Warm-up
Jog 5 minutes, active stretch, return, and active stretch.

Drills.
20 mtr:

     High knees x 4

     Heel flicks x 4

          High marching with a skip x 4

          Backwards running x 4

     4 x 20 mtr run through, sideways return

     High marching with skip and extension x 4

     Backwards running x 4

          Long skipping x 4 (10 mtrs)

          High skipping x 4 (10 mtrs)

     1 x 20 mtr run through

     Sideways return

     Active stretch

Hopping.
5 hops & a jump x 2 each leg
7 hops & a jump x 2 each leg
9 hops & a jump x 2 each leg

2 x 20 mtr run throughs walk back

Sprints.

Starts with various start positions (lying face down; push up; lying on back etc): 2 sets (6 x 30 mtr, 95% effort, walk back, 2 minute rest between repetitions), 5 minute rest between sets

Conditioning.

4 x 150mtr shuttles (15 x 2, 25 x 2, 35 x 2) work to rest ratio 1:3. Approx on 2 minutes.

Medicine ball circuit

Seated: Chest to chest x 25, overhead x 25; then repeat with legs in air.
Squat forward throws x 25
Underarm forward throw x 25
Rotations figure 8's x 10 each side
Under and over x 10

Recovery work & walk and wade. Gentle stretch.

Appendix 2

Water Polo: Sample Aerobic and Anaerobic sessions

I have provided the below swim workout session examples that I used in water polo to demonstrate the differences between aerobic and anaerobic programming. To note are the distances swum, rest periods and intensity, taken collectively. Even if you don't understand swimming per se, you should be able to appreciate the differences in program design associated with each area of physiology stress desired to be implemented.

Note: @ = time for each repetitions
       i = rest period between repetitions
      RI = rest period between sets
      FS = freestyle; BRS = breaststroke; FLY = Butterfly
      time eg: 1:25 =1 minute 25 seconds; 00:05 = 5 seconds

Aerobic session (endurance), total distance 5200 metres

Sets	Reps	Mtrs	Description	@	i	RI
1	1	300	FS	04:30	00:30	
1	1	300	FS + FLY kick	04:30	00:30	
1	1	300	100 FS kick + 100 FS + 100 FS kick	04:30	00:30	
1	1	300	FS pull	04:30	00:30	
4	5	200	FS: breathing 1st rep every 3; second rep every 4, then 3 and 4 again	02:30	00:20	07:00

Anaerobic session (sprint), total distance 3350 metres

Sets	Reps	Mtrs	Description	@	i	RI
1	1	400	4 x 100 reverse medley	10:00		
1	12	450	12.5 FS kick +25 FS	10:00		
1	5	100	25 FS K + 50 BRS effort +25 FS K max sprint	01:25	00:10	
5	1	50	FS max effort	00:30		3:00
1	1	200	Easy choice	04:00		
8	8	25	FS max, stop when time > 1st lap + 2 secs	00:14	00:05	04:00

www.ingramcontent.com/pod-product-compliance
Lightning Source LLC
Chambersburg PA
CBHW072140090426
42739CB00013B/3237